This book may be kept

DAS KARUSSELL *Drawn from a photograph*

RAINER
MARIA RILKE

FIFTY SELECTED POEMS

WITH ENGLISH TRANSLATIONS BY

C. F. MacINTYRE

Berkeley and Los Angeles · 1947

UNIVERSITY OF CALIFORNIA PRESS

UNIVERSITY OF CALIFORNIA PRESS

BERKELEY AND LOS ANGELES

CALIFORNIA

●

CAMBRIDGE UNIVERSITY PRESS

LONDON, ENGLAND

Second edition, second printing

PRINTED BY OFFSET IN THE UNITED STATES OF AMERICA

To
MY TEACHERS
at the University of Marburg

ACKNOWLEDGMENTS

I want to thank W. W. Norton & Company, publishers, of New York, for allowing me to publish translations of poems for which they hold the American copyrights: this permission was the more unusual because Mrs. M. D. Herter Norton has just done her own version of Rilke. I owe special thanks to her, because with a generosity hitherto unheard of in American letters she has been very helpful with suggestions and corrections; and we have given each other phrases and lines. Before these debts, I owe perhaps a greater one to Gustave Otto Arlt, without whose assistance there would have been no manuscript. The Editorial Committee of the University of California, especially Edward V. Brewer, gave me invaluable aid, and many friends saved me from minor pitfalls. Finally, Frau Ruth Sieber-Rilke let me see the poems in the poet's own hand and helped me with some of the notes.

C. F. M.

CONTENTS

CONTENTS

From NEUE GEDICHTE: ERSTER TEIL

From NEUE GEDICHTE: ANDERER TEIL

CONTENTS

INTRODUCTION

We murder to dissect.

AFTER I had got on with my personal Rilke for some ten years, I was surprised to discover I'd been living with a sort of Proteus who seems to have been all things to all critics and to have trifled with me,—even with the Nordic Diotima, Ellen Key, with the astute but vague Paul Valéry, and with the florid, oily Federico Olivero of the University of Turin. Every man had his own Rilke: to one he seems to have been the great God-seeker; to another, a Russian hermit with strong Gallic cultural antecedents; others saw him as a belated Eckhart or Tauler, a wearer of the diaphanous rags of Plotinus and Iamblichus, a spiritual bridegroom to the pious Mechtilde of Magdeburg; one ingenious person has hatched up for him a birth certificate as the only begotten son of the great lyrist Theodor Storm; yet another has placed him under the carved stony mantle of the French *Parnassiens*—and one quaint soul has found him, like a second Moses, floating among the faded bulrushes of the once lush Louise Labé. After some melancholy months of perturbation, during which time I have regarded his disaffections as personal disloyalty, I have been able to put most of these Rilkes aside in my mind (for future consideration), and to press their discoverers, or inventors, safely between "the leaves of the dark book" of German criticism which has been written despite the Olympian Lessing.

I want now to isolate my own Rilke, with a documented brief for his existence, as a man who during a certain period of his life rode the twin fillies of the wing'd horse, sculpture and painting, keeping a firm foot on each, and singing, as he went, his beautifully formed and colored sonnets, or polishing and painting small concert and salon pieces, sonatas in miniature. When he gallops out of the tent into the night of the soul in the *Duineser Elegien* and into the foggy obfuscations of *Die Sonette an Orpheus,* my blessing but not my interest goes with him, and I am, as yet, unconcerned with his after-fate. The illusion of his performance has been consummate, and it is the well-nigh perfect artist of three books whom I would present to my reader.

The poet of the period 1900–1908 seems to me, rather arbitrarily perhaps, to be the center of a circle drawn through three points: the painting of the Worpsweders and the French Impressionists, the sculpture of Rodin, and the poetry of Baudelaire, Verlaine, Mallarmé, and other Symbolists. The poems of *Das Buch der Bilder* and of the two parts of the *Neue Gedichte* represent an increasingly richer alloy of these various elements, until finally what the poet observes of form and color is expressed in a thin, clear music which is certainly not the German of the philologists. After he finished the last of these books, a great artist began to grow dim; the powerful filament from which light with the minimum of heat had emanated began to quiver forebodingly toward extinction.

In 1900 he went to Worpswede and lived for a time in the colony of painters. The following year he brought his wife Clara (nee Westhoff), one of Rodin's pupils, a sculptress whose masterpiece, their daughter Ruth, was produced here, while Rilke wrote his monograph on the Worpswede painters. There are many letters covering this period, from which the following excerpt must serve: "*Dank thun* will ich euch allen und eurem Lande und eurer Kunst" (letter to Otto Modersohn, one of the most distinguished painters of the group).

In 1902 he met Rodin, whose secretary he later became, and about whom he wrote a book. Hours of watching the sculptor at his work impressed on the poet a strong sense of the unity of a thing in bronze or stone. A painting can never possess the same vital existence as a plastic form standing alone in space; this viable reality is a quality of Rilke's best lyrics. That his association with Rodin influenced him greatly is shown by his many poems on statues and architecture: two on Apollo, three on the Buddha, the group on the cathedral at Chartres, other pieces on the Roman sarcophagi and fountain, and on the various buildings and squares of several cities. The last book ends with a poem on the stone scarabs and another done under stimulation of a statue of the Buddha,—although it is true that these, as finale, have transcended in the vastness of their conception any attempt to shut them in a half-ounce of carved pebble or even in a ton of bronze or black marble.

The works conceived from paintings or based on the art would make a no less impressive list: the Pietà, Saint Sebastian, the angels, Leda, a doge, a portrait of a lady, those of himself and his father, and in one poem, "Der Berg" (*Sechsunddreissig-mal und hundertmal / hat der Maler jenen Berg geschrieben*), he seems to give a fillip at the art itself. In his many poems on flowers and animals there is profound evidence that he observed nature with eyes that took note of form, color, and texture until at last he does not so much describe the object as make the reader see it for himself, projecting it from his own mind, as on a screen. This power to make a headlock on the reader and force his gaze in one direction only, Rilke got from wrestling with the technique of the sculptors and painters.

Let me now indicate the third point through which the circle limiting his art during this period was drawn. In the pages of

Die Aufzeichnungen des Malte Laurids Brigge will be found several references to various modern French poets; he made translations from Maurice de Guérin, André Gide, Paul Valéry, and Stéphane Mallarmé, and often the tone, approach, and feeling of his poems are reminiscent of the best of French poetry of the time.

Let the poet himself speak of his work:

Alas, those verses one writes in youth aren't much. One should wait and gather sweetness and light all his life, a long one if possible, and then maybe at the end he might write ten good lines. For poetry isn't, as people imagine, merely feelings (these come soon enough); it is experiences. To write one line, a man ought to see many cities, people, and things; he must learn to know animals and the way of birds in the air, and how little flowers open in the morning. One must be able to think back the way to unknown places ... and to partings long foreseen, to days of childhood ... and to parents ... to days on the sea ... to nights of travel ... and one must have memories of many nights of love, no two alike ... and the screams of women in childbed ... one must have sat by the dying, one must have sat by the dead in a room with open windows. ... But it is not enough to have memories. One must be able to forget them and have vast patience until they come again ... and when they become blood within us, and glances and gestures ... then first it can happen that in a rare hour the first word of a verse may arise and come forth ...

(*Malte*, pp. 25–27)

This condensation contains much of Rilke's theory of poetics; this is what he was thinking "up five flights of stairs, on a gray afternoon in Paris."

The most important poet in Germany since Goethe, let him be considered at this period of his life as a man who felt himself in exile, a man who spent his days in museums, galleries, studios, libraries, public parks and gardens; a wanderer of the streets by night, often even of the more sinister boulevards, a brooder on the many bridges over the Seine. He knew, as did Ovid of the *Tristia,* Tu Fu, Dante, and the later Heine, the bitterness of going up and down the stairs in the houses of others. He was a man of vast sympathy for the unfortunate and the disinherited: the blind, the cripples, the beggars, the suicides in the morgue, the harlots, the old maids, the animals in captivity—as an interpreter of animals he yields place to none,—and he understood the mysteries of childhood and the delicate nuances in the feelings of women.

And now he sits in an armchair, covered with rusty green, with gray greasy hollows pressed by dozens of heads, breathing the fumes of a *tête de moineau* which requires a quarter-hour's stoking: this man who dines at creameries, sickened by the smell of urine and the gray nasty reek of potatoes in stale grease: here he sits and dreams of Apollo, cathedrals with beautiful rose windows, charming little gazelles, angels, elderly spinsters brooding futilely in libraries, aristocratic ladies playing the piano, and of the Buddha sitting calmly on the lotus of contemplation.

Much has been and must yet be written of Rilke's technique and form, but he has packed the best analysis of creative power in one sentence:

Your blood drove you not to form nor to speak, but to reveal.

(*Malte,* p. 100)

I believe it was Zeuxis who painted grapes so realistically that the finches flew down and pecked at the canvas. Here was the proof of a splendid technique! But there was a Chinese Taoist (his name eludes me) who painted a crane (*Grus chinensis*) on an inn wall which had been plastered with cow dung—the picture was done in payment of his wine bill—and then suddenly mounted on the bird's back and flew off into the blue, leaving the wall as blank and bare as the innkeeper's face! This was the creation of *form* to the *n*th power. And Rilke's method of work-ing is almost the same; he creates the image of the object, stroke by meticulous stroke, and infuses life into the result by sudden revelation, the exact essence of which is not to be pronged by any critical scalpel.

This faculty he possesses in common with all poets, but to a greater degree than most of them. Perhaps I can best demon-strate his peculiar application of it and at the same time insert an opening wedge for my pet thesis by dissecting four of his animal poems and pointing out his several methods of approach.

In "Die Gazelle" (p. 64), at the first word, "verzauberte," one is immediately rapt into a magic world in such sharp con-trast to that suggested by the Latin name which subtitles the poem that the very shock whets the attention. If the rapidly suc-ceeding images seem at first to be entirely unrelated to gazelle, once you have noted and accepted the premise that the poet— after the first direct address to the animal—is really talking over with himself the artistic problem of the impossibility of catching the live beauty of the creature in two rhymed words, the rest of it will go off quite naturally, and each figure of speech will lead the next on to the stage by the hand, as children do at a Sunday School cantata. To proceed: these rhymes come and go, like a signal winking off and on (not bad, that, for the alternate move-ments of the animal's legs). Not only are the metaphors of the lyre and the branches rising from the gazelle's forehead *just* evocative comparisons, when the musical curves of the horns are considered, but a similar pair may very well have served as the frame for the first lyre. And since the branches suggest the laurel, another essential of the song god's equipment, Apollo might logically have been the recipient of this little monologue on the theory of poetry. This reference continues through the love songs with words as soft as rose petals. No one can complain about that; for the animal may have been standing conveniently before a rosebush—possibly the astute curators of the Botanical Gardens of Paris had provided an occasional floral nibble for the occupants. But mark how the petals fall on the tired eyelids of the reader: the poet himself with his eternal books, who suddenly conjures up (*verzauberte*) before the mind, which sees into the life of things, this creature of the imagination—not at all like Blake's symbolical tiger—through an odd and untranslatable pun. "Lauf" means both the leg of an animal and a gun barrel; this is merely a matter of language, and the poet didn't have to make it. But the metaphor is easily carried on by "charged but not fired," which makes the gazelle stand alertly on slender legs, "cocked" you might add, and ready for instant flight. Nor is this delicate suspension released by the final trope of the sonnet; for the poem ends with the seemingly completely foreign picture of a girl bathing in a forest pool. But then a girl, especially a German girl, might well have as much natural modesty as any nicely brought-up little gazelle! And there is a splendid suggestion of coyness in the reflection of the water on the half-averted face, with even a blush, maybe. Nevertheless, the reader is not to be diverted by the poet's caprice, and his mind instantly returns to the animal, posed against eternity, as real and beyond change as the bison on the walls of the caves at Altamira. And all this without any photographic description of the object. There is none of the veterinary's exposition of the stallion of Adonis. It is done calmly. No stars throw down their spears. No God directs its solitary flight. But one has seen a gazelle that never was on sea or land: Rilke's private little antelope, which now becomes the reader's forever. The next time you see one, you will notice that you get the same effect as from a doubly exposed negative, and that the poet's image is imposed on, and probably completely invests, your own picture. If this explanation has grown slightly longer than the fourteen lines of the original, it shows, as by a chart, the poet's power of compression. His figures are not the result of heliographic mirrors flashing bright thoughts from distant hills; they are the hitherto unapprehended facets of the crystal of his thought which are suddenly lighted by a fluoroscope.

In "Der Panther" (p. 62) he is concerned with another type of study. From the first he is dealing with nothing but the animal. There is only one figure of speech in the poem. These sharp notes were written by one who had watched the compact, softly moving beasts many times. There is the unusual observation of the nictitating membrane, common to the cat family, as it moves across the eyeball. Other translators have rendered this "eyelid." I have interviewed three panthers about this, but have got no results. After the dance of strength around the circle of the cage, no other action seems possible. Then it is that Rilke gets inside the panther (as Jupiter in the swan in the Leda poem) and looks out through the bars. Suddenly a picture—he does not say what, but one imagines the jungle forest and the pantheress—glides into the animal's eyes, flows through the tense body, and ceases in the heart. Mrs. M. D. Herter Norton calls this "one of the most dramatic moments in poetry." This animal is by no means Rilke's panther as the gazelle is his. This is Rilke *in* a panther, not fierce, but resigned with the sorrow of a dumb beast. Although it is not so hard to follow as the other animal poems, it probably represents a more complete embodiment of the poet's self in the object under consideration.

When he purposes a symbolic use of an animal, as in "Der Schwan" (p. 68), it is characteristic of the poet that he does not overdo his symbolism. He does full justice to the awkward movement of the bird on land, its clumsy descent into the water (which I have rendered by a literal compound of three words), and finally to the majestic natatory triumph with which the now very dignified bird moves—almost as if he (like the Queen of Spain) had no legs. Only as one thinks back does the full significance of the poem take effect: one has seen a pageant of life and death. The piece is not so pleasing as "The Gazelle," nor so moving as "The Panther," but it has its roots in a more universal human significance.

Still another treatment of a similar subject, this time more in the style of the painters, is found in "Die Flamingos" (p. 116). The luminous colors of Fragonard, one of the most delicate of the French painters, present the white, black, and fruit-red plumage above the rosy stilt-legs standing in sedge and flags: the whole thing like a bright flowerbed just outside the window—so immediately does he bring the picture before the reader. Moreover, here are two delicate glimpses of the soft beauty of woman: "she lay there, flushed with sleep," and the evocative name of the loveliest of the Greek hetaerae, Phryne, who was the model for statues by Praxiteles and paintings by Apelles—a whole gallery of fine young women, all appropriately white and rosy, and standing, perhaps, also in water, like the flamingos. By an extension of association the whole festival of the birth of Aphrodite is called forth, as the most glamorous girl in Hellas rises beautifully from the white sea foam ... and all the old men tremble. But the poet does not let one lose himself in artistic and erotic contemplation. Swiftly he hales the reader into a passionate and sympathetic participation in the futility of the caged birds which waken, stretch themselves, and soar through imaginary skies. The last three lines are master punches on a glass chin: a fine poetic shock. And there is nothing here about "only God can make a flamingo." There is, I believe, in all Rilke no reminiscence of the Landseer or the Rosa Bonheur school of faithful and sentimental animal painting. Only Whistler, or any one of the great Oriental artists a thousand years ago, or Monet could have painted these birds. Here the sensitive artist, lost in the love of living beauty, enriches it with images from the past, then, at the first note of suffering from his models, immediately becomes the seer vividly presenting the inner, deeper pain which is the essence of all beauty.

Perhaps these brief studies of his several methods of approaching a subject will suffice to indicate that one may expect a constant variety of concept and treatment in the poems. You've got already a very unusual little menagerie, as sharply differentiated as an ebony elephant from Ceylon, a carnelian mandarin duck, a French bronze stag, a Chelsea pottery poodle, a Mayan obsidian plumed serpent, or a Lalique glass colt.

This striking power of making the reader see through the poet's eyes is characteristic of the *Neue Gedichte;* but *Das Buch der Bilder,* although it represents Rilke as a mature artist, is too subjective, too full of ego-lyrics. It was written while he was still under the influence of the folk song and the traditional pastoral poetry of Germany. His vocabulary is limited, the verse is loose and capriciously handled, with stanzas and lines of varying length, with often a thirteen-line poem where he obviously purposed three quatrains but ran over the edge; and there are pieces which started to be sonnets but ended one line short or over. There is even a poem in terza rima which has a single isolated line and an interpolated quatrain. (I have not hesitated to reproduce this ragged effect in some of the translations from the first book.) His figures of speech lack the impact he developed in the later poems. One might say that in the former the soul looks out of itself at the world, and the poems are built on its reaction; in the more mature new poems a mind looks through an eye into the object, and the poems after describing the external, universal attributes go into the *Ding an sich*. My interest in Rilke's earlier work was stimulated largely by a desire to get a running start at the finished artist. In the *Neue Gedichte* he achieves a tightness of form, a progression to a climax, and a greater ability not to mold external figures but to pull the internal figures out of the poem itself. Here is no gesso work, no protrusion of added foreign matter into space beyond the canvas, like the glass jewels on the pictures of Carlo Crivelli; the poems have now the implicit depth and rotundity of Cézanne's apples. He is no longer a writer of subjective lyrics, but has become a painter and a seer.

Rilke's figures are his forte. They are never dragged along like trailers, nor fabricated to make his poetry pretty, as are those in Shelley's "Skylark." After all, this hidden poet—what is he hiding from?—this high-born maiden in a substantial thousand-ton tower—this golden glowworm in a dell of dew, admittedly all wet—what have these to do with the skylark? And if there is anything which a skylark is emphatically not like, it is a rose, probably pink, an undersized and sentimentally flushed cabbage! This sort of stuff is an excrescence on the legitimate body of English poetry and should be abated. Shelley has industriously lugged in four little similes, rolled them thin as piecrust, and made his poem twenty lines longer. These figures are the product of fancy, as Coleridge has defined it: the silver paper, the strung cranberries, the glass gewgaws, the popcorn balls, the tinsel angels stuck on the Christmas tree. Rilke's tropes are the brown tight cones, the legitimate fruit of a tree with roots in earth; they represent the power of true imagination which unfolds and develops from within. Resultants of the life force which is common to trees and poems, they are organic and not fabricated.

And, speaking of a tree, here is a fine chance to bring in his first poem, "Initiation," where the poet addresses you—"whoever you are"—and instructs you to go out and erect a tree before the evening sky. "And you have made the world." Your own world, your representation . . . and so on, to the last poem, "The Buddha in the Glory," where the almond *is* the Buddha, full, sweetly ripening, with its very shell extending to infinity. There is a directness of impact in these metaphors which is far beyond the circumlocutions of simile. Let me list other examples of comparisons which are likewise part and parcel of the work at hand: Apollo *is* the morning gazing through the leafless trees of spring; the Buddha (p. 61), with a woman's creative force, *is* in labor for a million years; and the thirsty king who picks up just any glass is likened to destiny "which also has a thirst"; the eyebrows of the Venetian courtesan resemble the bridges arched above the canals intimate with the sea; the balustrades crumbling at Versailles remind the poet of the former courtiers who bowed to the lonely king; and in another poem the harlot waits to seize one's hand—as if to wrap it in a dirty picked-up piece of paper; but the happily conceived simile likening the Spanish dancer to a flaring match is perhaps his most completely unified comparison, for the poem is built of some half-dozen allusions to fire. Truly, his figures are designed to "startle and waylay" the reader.

Regarding the present translations: the earlier book from which I have worked is written often in the folk-song measures which have influenced every German poet from Herder to

Heine, and the poems are slighter and easier to reproduce. But the two parts of the *Neue Gedichte* are mountain peaks, real and solid against clear sky. Unfortunately, he seems to have used these as a springboard for a leap toward an uncertain stratosphere; for his later books are to be followed only by inquisitive travelers in little air-tight mystical balloons. My choice of his three central books implies no criticism of his other work; but he is nowhere else so finished an artist. Anyone interested in writing will profit from a close study of the originals. The transmutation of German poetry into English verse is not quite so simple a matter as the kinship of the two languages might lead one to believe. Rilke's vocabulary includes archaic, neologic, and coined words. His punctuation is arbitrary and often inconsistent. His syntax leaves even his compatriots gasping—I have often foundered completely. The often purposed vagueness of the poems is exasperatingly created by his overuse of indefinite pronouns, many verbs either colorless or used in a secondary meaning, and his blessed relative clauses, which have been my despair. I have not hesitated to avail myself of his various metrical resources: variations from the fixed forms of verse, the use of a short line in an unexpected place, ellipsis of connectives, assonance and dissonance when an effect is required. Often I have been able to duplicate his devices; often again, I have used his bolder technique for the rendition of perfectly orthodox passages. For this liberty I can plead only that Goethe's remark to Eckermann, in 1831, influenced me profoundly: "If I were young and reckless enough, I would violate all the dicta of these critical gentlemen. I would use false rhyme, alliteration, and assonance, according to my caprice—but I would take care to say so many good things that everyone would read and remember them." Rilke has supplied me with the latter.

The following versions of the poems are the results of my anatomy lessons: crude drawings made while the eye, attentive over a microscope, gazed into something rich and strange. Rilke is an explosive experience. From "Initiation" to the final "The Buddha in the Glory" I have repeatedly undergone a progressive series of emotional effects which are climactic, like those of a symphony. And it is as music that Rilke is best approached; let the reader give himself to the rhythm, the melody, and the exaltation of the poems; the understanding will follow. His very oddities should be apprehended as the dissonances employed by all the great iconoclasts from Debussy to Schönberg, from Cézanne to Picasso. These three books rise to a mighty finale of surrender, like Beethoven's "Résignation! quel triste refuge! et pourtant c'est le seul qui me reste," to the awe of the last line, a silent thunder-crash, a flood of calm and penetrating light, worthy to stand beside

Das Ewig-Weibliche
Zieht uns hinan.

I have endeavored to correct in this edition a few mistakes to which my attention has been directed by Babette Deutsch, Jenny Ballou, and W. H. Auden. Had E. L. Stahl of Oxford been equally explicit, I should have attempted to expunge other mistranslations or additions. At least I hope to please him by adding that I have done the *Duineser Elegien* three times and am patiently waiting until the holders of the American copyrights allow me to hunt for a publisher. This hope constitutes a retraction of the unfortunate sentence on page 2.

Berkeley
1941

C. F. MacIntyre

... the translation does not give back the full meaning, and he wants to show to young people the beautiful and real fragments of this massive and glorious language which has been fused and made pliable in such intense flame ... he warms himself again to his work. Now come evenings, fine, almost youthful evenings, like those of autumn, for instance, which bring with them such long calm nights. In his study the lamp burns late. He does not always bend over the pages; he often leans back, closing within his eyes a line he has read over and over, until its meaning flows into his very blood.

—*Die Aufzeichnungen des Malte Laurids Brigge* (p. 278)

From DAS BUCH DER BILDER

EINGANG

Wᴇʀ du auch seist: Am Abend tritt hinaus
aus deiner Stube, drin du alles weißt;
als letztes vor der Ferne liegt dein Haus:
Wer du auch seist.
Mit deinen Augen, welche müde kaum
von der verbrauchten Schwelle sich befrein,
hebst du ganz langsam einen schwarzen Baum
und stellst ihn vor den Himmel: schlank, allein.
Und hast die Welt gemacht. Und sie ist groß
und wie ein Wort, das noch im Schweigen reift.
Und wie dein Wille ihren Sinn begreift,
lassen sie deine Augen zärtlich los...

INITIATION

Whoever you are, go out into the evening,
leaving your room, of which you know each bit;
your house is the last before the infinite,
whoever you are.
Then with your eyes that wearily
scarce lift themselves from the worn-out door-stone
slowly you raise a shadowy black tree
and fix it on the sky: slender, alone.
And you have made the world (and it shall grow
and ripen as a word, unspoken, still).
When you have grasped its meaning with your will,
then tenderly your eyes will let it go ...

RITTER

REITET der Ritter in schwarzem Stahl
hinaus in die rauschende Welt.
Und draußen ist alles: der Tag und das Tal
und der Freund und der Feind und das Mahl im Saal
und der Mai und die Maid und der Wald und der Gral,
und Gott ist selber vieltausendmal
an alle Straßen gestellt.

Doch in dem Panzer des Ritters drinnen,
hinter den finstersten Ringen,
hockt der Tod und muß sinnen und sinnen:
Wann wird die Klinge springen
über die Eisenhecke,
die fremde befreiende Klinge,
die mich aus meinem Verstecke
holt, drin ich so viele
gebückte Tage verbringe,—
daß ich mich endlich strecke
und spiele
und singe.

THE KNIGHT

THE knight rides forth in sable mail
into the stirring world.
Out there is all:
the friend, the foe, the valley, the day,
the meal in the hall,
the maid and the wood and the month of May,
and the Holy Grail,
and God himself many thousand times
is shown in the streets.

Yet, in the armor of the knight,
behind the sinister rings,
Death squats, brooding and brooding:
When will the sword spring
over the hedge of iron,
that strange and freeing blade,
to fetch me from this place
that has cramped me many a day,
so that at last I can stretch myself
and sing
and play?

DER WAHNSINN

Sɪᴇ muß immer sinnen: Ich bin ... ich bin ...
Wer bist du denn, Marie?
  Eine Königin, eine Königin!
  In die Kniee vor mir, in die Knie!

Sie muß immer weinen: Ich war ... ich war ...
Wer warst du denn, Marie?
  Ein Niemandskind, ganz arm und bar,
  und ich kann dir nicht sagen wie.

Und wurdest aus einem solchen Kind
eine Fürstin, vor der man kniet?
  Weil die Dinge alle anders sind,
  als man sie beim Betteln sieht.

So haben die Dinge dich groß gemacht,
und kannst du noch sagen wann?
  Eine Nacht, eine Nacht, über eine Nacht,—
  und sie sprachen mich anders an.
  Ich trat in die Gasse hinaus und sieh:
  die ist wie mit Saiten bespannt;
  da wurde Marie Melodie, Melodie ...
  und tanzte von Rand zu Rand.
  Die Leute schlichen so ängstlich hin,
  wie hart an die Häuser gepflanzt,—
  denn das darf doch nur eine Königin,
  daß sie tanzt in den Gassen: tanzt! ...

MADNESS

She must ever brood: I am ... I am ...
Who are you then, Marie?
  I am a queen! I am a queen!
  On your knee there! On your knee!

She must ever weep: I was ... I was ...
Who were you then, Marie?
  A no one's child—I can't say how—
  but alone, in poverty.

And how could such a child become
a princess to whom one kneels?
  Because all things are different now
  from what a beggar feels.

So, things have raised you to such heights,
but you can't tell how or when?
  One night, one night, all in one night,
  they changed towards me then.
  I walked in the street and suddenly
  it was stretched with trembling strings.
  Marie became melody, melody ...
  and danced to their musicking.
  The people cowered fearfully,
  as if rooted by their feet.
  It's only a queen who dares to dance,
  yes, dance in a city street!

DIE ENGEL

Sɪᴇ haben alle müde Münde
und helle Seelen ohne Saum.
Und eine Sehnsucht (wie nach Sünde)
geht ihnen manchmal durch den Traum.

Fast gleichen sie einander alle;
in Gottes Gärten schweigen sie,
wie viele, viele Intervalle
in seiner Macht und Melodie.

Nur wenn sie ihre Flügel breiten,
sind sie die Wecker eines Winds:
Als ginge Gott mit seinen weiten
Bildhauerhänden durch die Seiten
im dunklen Buch des Anbeginns.

THE ANGELS

THEY all have weary mouths,
bright souls without a seam.
And a yearning (as for sin)
often haunts their dream.

They wander, each and each alike,
in God's garden silently,
as many, many intervals
in his might and melody.

Only when they spread their wings
they waken a great wind through the land:
as though with his broad sculptor-hands
God was turning
the leaves of the dark book of the Beginning.

AUS EINER KINDHEIT

Das Dunkeln war wie Reichtum in dem Raume,
darin der Knabe, sehr verheimlicht, saß.
Und als die Mutter eintrat wie im Traume,
erzitterte im stillen Schrank ein Glas.
Sie fühlte, wie das Zimmer sie verriet,
und küßte ihren Knaben: Bist du hier? . . .
Dann schauten beide bang nach dem Klavier,
denn manchen Abend hatte sie ein Lied,
darin das Kind sich seltsam tief verfing.

Es saß sehr still. Sein großes Schauen hing
an ihrer Hand, die ganz gebeugt vom Ringe,
als ob sie schwer in Schneewehn ginge,
über die weißen Tasten ging.

FROM A CHILDHOOD

THE darkness was a richness in the room
where the boy sat, hidden, by himself.
And when the mother entered, as in a dream,
a thin glass trembled on the silent shelf.
She felt as if the room betrayed her, but
she kissed her boy and murmured: Are you here?
Then both glanced shyly at the dark clavier,
for often in the evening she would sing
a song in which the child was strangely caught.

He sat so quietly, his gaze bent low
upon her hands, weighed down with heavy rings,
moving along the white keys as men go
heavily through deep drifts of snow.

DER NACHBAR

FREMDE Geige, gehst du mir nach?
In wieviel fernen Städten schon sprach
deine einsame Nacht zu meiner?
Spielen dich Hunderte? Spielt dich einer?

Gibt es in allen großen Städten
solche, die sich ohne dich
schon in den Flüssen verloren hätten?
Und warum trifft es immer mich?

Warum bin ich immer der Nachbar derer,
die dich bange zwingen zu singen
und zu sagen: Das Leben ist schwerer
als die Schwere von allen Dingen?

THE NEIGHBOR

Strange violin, are you following me?
In how many towns when I am alone
your lonely night has called to mine?
Do hundreds play you, or only one?

Are there in all great cities ever
those who without you would have lost
themselves already in the river?
Will your music pick on me to the last?

Why must I always have as neighbor
him who makes you fearfully sing
and say that life is heavier
than the heaviness of all things?

DER EINSAME

Wie einer, der auf fremden Meeren fuhr,
so bin ich bei den ewig Einheimischen;
die vollen Tage stehn auf ihren Tischen,
mir aber ist die Ferne voll Figur.

In mein Gesicht reicht eine Welt herein,
die vielleicht unbewohnt ist wie ein Mond,
sie aber lassen kein Gefühl allein,
und alle ihre Worte sind bewohnt.

Die Dinge, die ich weither mit mir nahm,
sehn selten aus, gehalten an das Ihre—:
in ihrer großen Heimat sind sie Tiere,
hier halten sie den Atem an vor Scham.

THE SOLITARY

As one who has sailed across an unknown sea,
among this rooted folk I am alone;
the full days on their tables are their own,
to me the distant is reality.

A new world reaches to my very eyes,
a place perhaps unpeopled as the moon;
their slightest feelings they must analyze,
and all their words have got the common tune.

The things I brought with me from far away,
compared with theirs, look strangely not the same:
in their great country they were living things,
but here they hold their breath, as if for shame.

KLAGE

O wie ist alles fern
und lange vergangen.
Ich glaube, der Stern,
von welchem ich Glanz empfange,
ist seit Jahrtausenden tot.
Ich glaube, im Boot,
das vorüberfuhr,
hörte ich etwas Banges sagen.
Im Hause hat eine Uhr
geschlagen...
In welchem Haus?...
Ich möchte aus meinem Herzen hinaus
unter den großen Himmel treten.
Ich möchte beten.
Und einer von allen Sternen
müßte wirklich noch sein.
Ich glaube, ich wüßte,
welcher allein
gedauert hat,
welcher wie eine weiße Stadt
am Ende des Strahls in den Himmeln steht...

LAMENT

Oн, everything is far
and long ago.
I believe that star
these thousand years is dead,
though I still see its light.
I believe, in that boat
passing through the night
something fearful was said.
In the house a clock
struck ...
Where did it strike? ...
I would like to walk
out of my heart
under the wide sky.
I would like to pray.
One of all these stars
must still exist.
I believe I know
which one
still lasts
and stands like a city, white
in the sky at the end of the beam of light ...

EINSAMKEIT

Die Einsamkeit ist wie ein Regen.
Sie steigt vom Meer den Abenden entgegen;
von Ebenen, die fern sind und entlegen,
geht sie zum Himmel, der sie immer hat.
Und erst vom Himmel fällt sie auf die Stadt.

Regnet hernieder in den Zwitterstunden,
wenn sich nach Morgen wenden alle Gassen,
und wenn die Leiber, welche nichts gefunden,
enttäuscht und traurig voneinander lassen;
und wenn die Menschen, die einander hassen,
in einem Bett zusammen schlafen müssen:

dann geht die Einsamkeit mit den Flüssen...

SOLITUDE

SOLITUDE is like a rain.
It rises from the sea to meet the evening;
it rises from the dim, far-distant plain
toward the sky, as by an old birthright.
And thence falls on the city from the height.

It falls like rain in that gray doubtful hour
when all the streets are turning toward the dawn,
and when those bodies, with all hope foregone
of what they sought, are sorrowfully alone;
and when all men, who hate each other, creep
together in one common bed for sleep;

then solitude flows onward with the rivers...

HERBSTTAG

HERR: es ist Zeit. Der Sommer war sehr groß.
Leg deinen Schatten auf die Sonnenuhren,
und auf den Fluren laß die Winde los.

Befiehl den letzten Früchten voll zu sein;
gib ihnen noch zwei südlichere Tage,
dränge sie zur Vollendung hin und jage
die letzte Süße in den schweren Wein.

Wer jetzt kein Haus hat, baut sich keines mehr.
Wer jetzt allein ist, wird es lange bleiben,
wird wachen, lesen, lange Briefe schreiben
und wird in den Alleen hin und her
unruhig wandern, wenn die Blätter treiben.

AUTUMN DAY

Lord, it is time. The summer was too long.
Lay now thy shadow over the sundials,
and on the meadows let the winds blow strong.

Bid the last fruit to ripen on the vine;
allow them still two friendly southern days
to bring them to perfection and to force
the final sweetness in the heavy wine.

Who has no house now will not build him one.
Who is alone now will be long alone,
will waken, read, and write long letters
and through the barren pathways up and down
restlessly wander when dead leaves are blown.

ERINNERUNG

UND du wartest, erwartest das Eine,
das dein Leben unendlich vermehrt;
das Mächtige, Ungemeine,
das Erwachen der Steine,
Tiefen, dir zugekehrt.

Es dämmern im Bücherständer
die Bände in Gold und Braun;
und du denkst an durchfahrene Länder,
an Bilder, an die Gewänder
wiederverlorener Fraun.

Und da weißt du auf einmal: Das war es.
Du erhebst dich, und vor dir steht
eines vergangenen Jahres
Angst und Gestalt und Gebet.

MEMORY

AND you wait, awaiting the one
to make your small life grow:
the mighty, the uncommon,
the awakening of stone,
the depths to be opened below.

Now duskily in the bookcase
gleam the volumes in brown and gold;
you remember lands you have wandered through,
the pictures and the garments
of women lost of old.

And you suddenly know: It was here!
You pull yourself together, and there
stands an irrevocable year
of anguish and vision and prayer.

ENDE DES HERBSTES

Ich sehe seit einer Zeit,
wie alles sich verwandelt.
Etwas steht auf und handelt
und tötet und tut Leid.

Von Mal zu Mal sind all
die Gärten nicht dieselben;
von den gilbenden zu der gelben
langsamen Verfall:
wie war der Weg mir weit.

Jetzt bin ich bei den leeren
und schaue durch alle Alleen.
Fast bis zu den fernen Meeren
kann ich den ernsten schweren
verwehrenden Himmel sehn.

END OF AUTUMN

I have seen for some time now
the change in everything.
Something arises and acts
and kills and brings suffering.

In the gardens now from day to day
is a change from green
to yellow and gray,
a slow dying-away:
how long my road has been.

Now I stand in this emptiness
and look down the rows of trees.
Almost to the distant sea
the foreboding earnestness
of the sky lies heavily.

HERBST

Dɪᴇ Blätter fallen, fallen wie von weit,
als welkten in den Himmeln ferne Gärten;
sie fallen mit verneinender Gebärde.

Und in den Nächten fällt die schwere Erde
aus allen Sternen in die Einsamkeit.

Wir alle fallen. Diese Hand da fällt.
Und sieh dir andre an: es ist in allen.

Und doch ist Einer, welcher dieses Fallen
unendlich sanft in seinen Händen hält.

AUTUMN

THE leaves fall, fall as if from far away,
like withered things from gardens deep in sky;
they fall with gestures of renunciation.

And through the night the heavy earth falls too,
down from the stars, into the loneliness.

And we all fall. This hand must fall.
Look everywhere: it is the lot of all.

Yet there is one who holds us as we fall
eternally in his hands' tenderness.

ABEND

DER Abend wechselt langsam die Gewänder,
die ihm ein Rand von alten Bäumen hält;
du schaust: und von dir scheiden sich die Länder,
ein himmelfahrendes und eins, das fällt;

und lassen dich, zu keinem ganz gehörend,
nicht ganz so dunkel wie das Haus, das schweigt,
nicht ganz so sicher Ewiges beschwörend
wie das, was Stern wird jede Nacht und steigt;

und lassen dir (unsäglich zu entwirrn)
dein Leben, bang und riesenhaft und reifend,
so daß es, bald begrenzt und bald begreifend,
abwechselnd Stein in dir wird und Gestirn.

EVENING

SLOWLY now the evening changes his garments
held for him by a rim of ancient trees;
you gaze: and the landscape divides and leaves you,
one sinking and one rising toward the sky.

And you are left, to none belonging wholly,
not so dark as a silent house, nor quite
so surely pledged unto eternity
as that which grows to star and climbs the night.

To you is left (unspeakably confused)
your life, gigantic, ripening, full of fears,
so that it, now hemmed in, now grasping all,
is changed in you by turns to stone and stars.

ERNSTE STUNDE

WER jetzt weint irgendwo in der Welt,
ohne Grund weint in der Welt,
weint über mich.

Wer jetzt lacht irgendwo in der Nacht,
ohne Grund lacht in der Nacht,
lacht mich aus.

Wer jetzt geht irgendwo in der Welt,
ohne Grund geht in der Welt,
geht zu mir.

Wer jetzt stirbt irgendwo in der Welt,
ohne Grund stirbt in der Welt,
sieht mich an.

SOLEMN HOUR

Who weeps now anywhere in the world,
without cause weeps in the world,
weeps over me.

Who laughs now anywhere in the night,
without cause laughs in the night,
laughs at me.

Who goes now anywhere in the world,
without cause goes in the world,
goes to me.

Who dies now anywhere in the world,
without cause dies in the world,
looks at me.

STROPHEN

Ist einer, der nimmt alle in die Hand,
daß sie wie Sand durch seine Finger rinnen.
Er wählt die schönsten aus den Königinnen
und läßt sie sich in weißen Marmor hauen,
still liegend in des Mantels Melodie;
und legt die Könige zu ihren Frauen,
gebildet aus dem gleichen Stein wie sie.

Ist einer, der nimmt alle in die Hand,
daß sie wie schlechte Klingen sind und brechen.
Er ist kein Fremder, denn er wohnt im Blut,
das unser Leben ist und rauscht und ruht.
Ich kann nicht glauben, daß er unrecht tut;
doch hör ich viele Böses von ihm sprechen.

STROPHES

THERE is one who takes all within his hand,
lets them run through his fingers, even as sand;
he chooses the most beautiful of queens
and has them carved in whitest marble stone,
lying stilly in the mantel's melody;
he bids the kings laid by their wives to be
hewn from exactly the same stone as they.

There is one who takes all within his hand,
that they like badly tempered swords be broken.
He is no stranger, but lives in the blood
which is our life, now resting, now in flood.
I cannot credit that he can do wrong,
though I have heard much evil of him spoken.

DAS LIED DER WAISE

Ich bin niemand und werde auch niemand sein.
Jetzt bin ich ja zum Sein noch zu klein;
aber auch später.

Mütter und Väter,
erbarmt euch mein.

Zwar es lohnt nicht des Pflegens Müh:
ich werde doch gemäht.
Mich kann keiner brauchen: jetzt ist es zu früh,
und morgen ist es zu spät.

Ich habe nur dieses eine Kleid,
es wird dünn, und es verbleicht,
aber es hält eine Ewigkeit
auch noch vor Gott vielleicht.

Ich habe nur dieses bißchen Haar
(immer dasselbe blieb),
das einmal Eines Liebstes war.

Nun hat er nichts mehr lieb.

THE SONG OF THE WAIF

I am nobody and always will be.
I'm almost too little to live, right now,
and even later.

O mothers and fathers,
have pity on me.

But it's not worth your bother:
I'll still be mowed down.
No one can use me: it's too early. Wait
until tomorrow—then it's too late.

I've only this little gown,
and it's getting thin and faded . . .
but it holds an eternity,
and even before God, maybe.

I've only this lock from her brow
(it stays always the same),
it was father's treasure once.

He doesn't love anything now.

AUS EINER STURMNACHT

VI

In solchen Nächten sind alle die Städte gleich,
alle beflaggt.
Und an den Fahnen vom Sturm gepackt
und wie an Haaren hinausgerissen
in irgendein Land mit ungewissen
Umrissen und Flüssen.
In allen Gärten ist dann ein Teich,
an jedem Teiche dasselbe Haus,
in jedem Hause dasselbe Licht;
und alle Menschen sehn ähnlich aus
und halten die Hände vorm Gesicht.

VIII

In solchen Nächten wächst mein Schwesterlein,
das vor mir war und vor mir starb, ganz klein.
Viel solche Nächte waren schon seither:
Sie muß schon schön sein. Bald wird irgendwer
    sie frein.

FROM A STORMY NIGHT

VI

On nights like this all cities are alike,
with cloud-flags hung.
The banners by the storm are flung,
torn out like hair
in any country anywhere
whose boundaries and rivers are uncertain.
In every garden is a pond,
the same little house sits just beyond;
the same light is in all the houses;
and all the people look alike
and hold their hands before their faces.

VIII

On nights like this my little sister grows,
who was born and died before me, very small.
There have been many such nights, gone long ago:
she must be lovely now. Soon the suitors will call.

From NEUE GEDICHTE: ERSTER TEIL

KARL UND ELISABETH VON DER HEYDT
IN FREUNDSCHAFT

FRÜHER APOLLO

Wie manches Mal durch das noch unbelaubte
Gezweig ein Morgen durchsieht, der schon ganz
im Frühling ist: so ist in seinem Haupte
nichts, was verhindern könnte, daß der Glanz

aller Gedichte uns fast tödlich träfe;
denn noch kein Schatten ist in seinem Schaun,
zu kühl für Lorbeer sind noch seine Schläfe,
und später erst wird aus den Augenbrau'n

hochstämmig sich der Rosengarten heben,
aus welchem Blätter, einzeln, ausgelöst
hintreiben werden auf des Mundes Beben,

der jetzt noch still ist, niegebraucht und blinkend
und nur mit seinem Lächeln etwas trinkend,
als würde ihm sein Singen eingeflößt.

EARLY APOLLO

As, many times between the leafless limbs
a morning looks out, which already stands
wholly in spring: so this stone head commands
that nothing hinder the bright glow or dim

the fatal splendor of the poem's blow;
for yet no shadow lingers on his gaze;
his temples are too cool to need the bay,
and only later, thrust forth from his brow,

rich roses shall arise, on proud tall stems:
flowers whose petals, singly loosed, shall fall
slowly on his young mouth's quivering,

his mouth, yet firm, unused but shimmering
with a faint smile which drinks to have its fill
as if his song were being transfused in him.

OPFER

O wie blüht mein Leib aus jeder Ader
duftender, seitdem ich dich erkenn;
sieh, ich gehe schlanker und gerader,
und du wartest nur–: wer bist du denn?

Sieh: ich fühle, wie ich mich entferne,
wie ich Altes, Blatt um Blatt, verlier.
Nur dein Lächeln steht wie lauter Sterne
über dir und bald auch über mir.

Alles was durch meine Kinderjahre
namenlos noch und wie Wasser glänzt,
will ich nach dir nennen am Altare,
der entzündet ist von deinem Haare
und mit deinen Brüsten leicht bekränzt.

OBLATION

Oh, how my body blooms from every vein,
more fragrant, since you came into my ken.
See how I walk, more slender and upright,
and you wait calmly—and who are you, then?

Behold: I feel that I have left me far
behind and shed my old life, leaf by leaf,
till finally there is nothing but the star
of your smile shining richly on our life.

Everything that through my childhood years
was nameless still and glistening like water
I will christen after you before the altar,
which is made radiant by your shining hair,
the altar which your breasts have lightly crowned.

BUDDHA

ALS ob er horchte. Stille: eine Ferne...
Wir halten ein und hören sie nicht mehr.
Und er ist Stern. Und andre große Sterne,
die wir nicht sehen, stehen um ihn her.

O er ist alles. Wirklich, warten wir,
daß er uns sähe? Sollte er bedürfen?
Und wenn wir hier uns vor ihm niederwürfen,
er bliebe tief und träge wie ein Tier.

Denn das, was uns zu seinen Füßen reißt,
das kreist in ihm seit Millionen Jahren.
Er, der vergißt, was wir erfahren,
und der erfährt, was uns verweist.

THE BUDDHA

As if he listened. Silence, far and far . . .
we draw back till we hear its depths no more.
And he is star. And other giant stars
which we cannot see stand about him here.

Oh, he is all. And really, do we wait
till he shall see us? Has he need of that?
Even should we throw ourselves before him,
he would be deep, and indolent as a cat.

He has been in labor for a million years
with this which pulls us to his very feet.
He who forgets that which we must endure,
who knows what is withdrawn beyond our fate.

DER PANTHER
IM JARDIN DES PLANTES, PARIS

SEIN Blick ist vom Vorübergehn der Stäbe
so müd geworden, daß er nichts mehr hält.
Ihm ist, als ob es tausend Stäbe gäbe
und hinter tausend Stäben keine Welt.

Der weiche Gang geschmeidig starker Schritte,
der sich im allerkleinsten Kreise dreht,
ist wie ein Tanz von Kraft um eine Mitte,
in der betäubt ein großer Wille steht.

Nur manchmal schiebt der Vorhang der Pupille
sich lautlos auf—. Dann geht ein Bild hinein,
geht durch der Glieder angespannte Stille—
und hört im Herzen auf zu sein.

THE PANTHER

JARDIN DES PLANTES, PARIS

His sight from ever gazing through the bars
has grown so blunt that it sees nothing more.
It seems to him that thousands of bars are
before him, and behind them nothing merely.

The easy motion of his supple stride,
which turns about the very smallest circle,
is like a dance of strength about a center
in which a mighty will stands stupefied.

Only sometimes when the pupil's film
soundlessly opens . . . then one image fills
and glides through the quiet tension of the limbs
into the heart and ceases and is still.

DIE GAZELLE

ANTILOPE DORCAS

VERZAUBERTE: wie kann der Einklang zweier
erwählter Worte je den Reim erreichen,
der in dir kommt und geht, wie auf ein Zeichen.
Aus deiner Stirne steigen Laub und Leier,

und alles Deine geht schon im Vergleich
durch Liebeslieder, deren Worte, weich
wie Rosenblätter, dem, der nicht mehr liest,
sich auf die Augen legen, die er schließt,

um dich zu sehen: hingetragen, als
wäre mit Sprüngen jeder Lauf geladen
und schösse nur nicht ab, solang der Hals

das Haupt ins Horchen hält: wie wenn beim Baden
im Wald die Badende sich unterbricht,
den Waldsee im gewendeten Gesicht.

THE GAZELLE
DORCAS GAZELLE

ENCHANTED one: how shall two chosen words
achieve the harmony of the pure rhyme
which in you like a signal comes and goes?
From your forehead the leafy lyre climbs,

and all your being moves in sure accord,
like those love-lyrics whose words softly flow:
rose petals laid upon the closed eyelids
of one grown weary, who no longer reads

but shuts his eyes to see you—swiftly brought,
as though each leg were charged with leaps but not
fired, as long as the neck holds the head

quiet to listen: as when in a green place
a bather in the woods is interrupted . . .
with the lake's shine on her averted face.

RÖMISCHE SARKOPHAGE

Was aber hindert uns zu glauben, daß
(so wie wir hingestellt sind und verteilt)
nicht eine kleine Zeit nur Drang und Haß
und dies Verwirrende in uns verweilt,

wie einst in dem verzierten Sarkophag
bei Ringen, Götterbildern, Gläsern, Bändern,
in langsam sich verzehrenden Gewändern
ein langsam Aufgelöstes lag—

bis es die unbekannten Munde schluckten,
die niemals reden. (Wo besteht und denkt
ein Hirn, um ihrer einst sich zu bedienen?)

Da wurde von den alten Aquädukten
ewiges Wasser in sie eingelenkt—:
das spiegelt jetzt und geht und glänzt in ihnen.

ROMAN SARCOPHAGI

BUT what prevents us from believing that
(so we are parceled off here by division)
not for a short time only force and hate
and this confusion are our final portion:

as once in this adorned sarcophagus,
with rings and carven gods, ribbons and glasses,
in slowly rotting garments something passed,
slowly: a thing dissolved lay thus—

till it was swallowed by the unknown maws
that never speak. (Where shall arise a brain
to think for them and put them to some use?)

Then from the ancient aqueducts—oh, then
eternal water would be turned into them—:
which glitters there and goes and gleams again.

DER SCHWAN

Diese Mühsal, durch noch Ungetanes
schwer und wie gebunden hinzugehn,
gleicht dem ungeschaffnen Gang des Schwanes.

Und das Sterben, dieses Nichtmehrfassen
jenes Grunds, auf dem wir täglich stehn,
seinem ängstlichen Sich-Niederlassen—:

in die Wasser, die ihn sanft empfangen
und die sich, wie glücklich und vergangen,
unter ihm zurückziehn, Flut um Flut;
während er unendlich still und sicher
immer mündiger und königlicher
und gelassener zu ziehn geruht.

THE SWAN

THIS misery that through the still-undone
must pass, bound and heavily weighed down,
is like the awkward walking of the swan.

And death, where we no longer comprehend
the very ground on which we daily stand,
is like his anxious letting-himself-go

into the water, soft against his breast,
which now how easily together flows
behind him in a little wake of waves ...
while he, infinitely silent, self-possessed,
and ever more mature, is pleased to move
serenely on in his majestic way.

EIN FRAUENSCHICKSAL

So wie der König auf der Jagd ein Glas
ergreift, daraus zu trinken, irgendeines,—
und wie hernach der, welcher es besaß,
es fortstellt und verwahrt, als wär es keines:

so hob vielleicht das Schicksal, durstig auch,
bisweilen Eine an den Mund und trank,
die dann ein kleines Leben, viel zu bang
sie zu zerbrechen, abseits vom Gebrauch

hinstellte in die ängstliche Vitrine,
in welcher seine Kostbarkeiten sind
(oder die Dinge, die für kostbar gelten).

Da stand sie fremd wie eine Fortgeliehne
und wurde einfach alt und wurde blind
und war nicht kostbar und war niemals selten.

A WOMAN'S FATE

Even as a king out hunting seized a glass,
something to drink from—any glass, no matter,—
and someone after that in a sure place
put the slight thing away, to guard it better:

thus destiny, which also has a thirst,
picked up this woman, drank of her till slaked,
and afterward some trivial fellow durst
not put her to her use, for fear she break,

and stuck her in that careful cupboard where
one cherishes all costly things and rare
(or things that people fancy have some worth).

And there she stood, as strange as something loaned,
slowly growing merely old and blind,
and was not prized and never rare on earth.

BLAUE HORTENSIE

So wie das letzte Grün in Farbentiegeln
sind diese Blätter, trocken, stumpf und rauh,
hinter den Blütendolden, die ein Blau
nicht auf sich tragen, nur von ferne spiegeln.

Sie spiegeln es verweint und ungenau,
als wollten sie es wiederum verlieren,
und wie in alten blauen Briefpapieren
ist Gelb in ihnen, Violett und Grau;

Verwaschnes wie an einer Kinderschürze,
Nichtmehrgetragnes, dem nichts mehr geschieht:
wie fühlt man eines kleinen Lebens Kürze.

Doch plötzlich scheint das Blau sich zu verneuen
in einer von den Dolden, und man sieht
ein rührend Blaues sich vor Grünem freuen.

BLUE HYDRANGEAS

LIKE the last green in the palette's colors,
these leaves are without luster, rough and dry
under umbeled flowers that were duller
but for a blue reflected from the sky.

They mirror it, exhausted as with tears,
vaguely, as if not wishing it to stay;
as old blue letter-paper which the years
have touched with yellow, violet, and gray;

washed-out like a child's apron, no more used—
nothing else can happen to it now:
one feels how short the little life has been.

But suddenly the blue seems to renew
itself in one last cluster—and see how
the pathetic blue rejoices in the green.

VOR DEM SOMMERREGEN

Auf einmal ist aus allem Grün im Park
man weiß nicht was, ein Etwas, fortgenommen;
man fühlt ihn näher an die Fenster kommen
und schweigsam sein. Inständig nur und stark

ertönt aus dem Gehölz der Regenpfeifer,
man denkt an einen Hieronymus:
so sehr steigt irgend Einsamkeit und Eifer
aus dieser einen Stimme, die der Guß

erhören wird. Des Saales Wände sind
mit ihren Bildern von uns fortgetreten,
als dürften sie nicht hören, was wir sagen.

Es spiegeln die verblichenen Tapeten
das ungewisse Licht von Nachmittagen,
in denen man sich fürchtete als Kind.

BEFORE THE SUMMER RAIN

Suddenly in the park from all the green,
one knows not what, but something real is gone:
one feels it coming, silent and unseen,
toward the window. Urgently and strong,

out of the wood the dotterel implores—
until one thinks of Saint Jerome: such zeal
and loneliness rise in one voice, which shall
be answered when the rain begins to pour.

Now the walls and pictures of the room
grow dim, as if pushed suddenly away,
as if they dared not hear the words we say.

And on the faded hangings falls the chilled
uncertain light of afternoon: the gloom
in which one felt so frightened, as a child.

LETZTER ABEND

Und Nacht und fernes Fahren; denn der Train
des ganzen Heeres zog am Park vorüber.
Er aber hob den Blick vom Clavecin
und spielte noch und sah zu ihr hinüber

beinah, wie man in einen Spiegel schaut:
so sehr erfüllt von seinen jungen Zügen
und wissend, wie sie seine Trauer trügen,
schön und verführender bei jedem Laut.

Doch plötzlich wars, als ob sich das verwische:
sie stand wie mühsam in der Fensternische
und hielt des Herzens drängendes Geklopf.

Sein Spiel gab nach. Von draußen wehte Frische.
Und seltsam fremd stand auf dem Spiegeltische
der schwarze Tschako mit dem Totenkopf.

THE LAST EVENING

Night and the distant rumbling; for the train
of the whole army passed by the estate.
But still he raised his eyes and played again
the clavichord and gazed at her ... and waited,

almost like a man looking in a mirror
which was completely filled with his young face,
knowing how his features bore his sorrow,
more beautifully seductive with the grace

of music. The scene faded out. Instead,
wearily at the window, in her trouble,
she held the violent thumping of her heart.

He finished. The dawn wind was blowing hard.
And strangely alien on the mirror table
stood the black shako with the white death's-head.

DIE KURTISANE

Venedigs Sonne wird in meinem Haar
ein Gold bereiten: aller Alchemie
erlauchten Ausgang. Meine Brauen, die
den Brücken gleichen, siehst du sie

hinführen ob der lautlosen Gefahr
der Augen, die ein heimlicher Verkehr
an die Kanäle schließt, so daß das Meer
in ihnen steigt und fällt und wechselt. Wer

mich einmal sah, beneidet meinen Hund,
weil sich auf ihm oft in zerstreuter Pause
die Hand, die nie an keiner Glut verkohlt,

die unverwundbare, geschmückt, erholt—.
Und Knaben, Hoffnungen aus altem Hause,
gehn wie an Gift an meinem Mund zugrund.

THE COURTESAN

THE sun of Venice will prepare
with gracious alchemy gold in my hair:
a final triumph. And my slender brows
resemble bridges—can you not see how

they span the silent danger of my eyes
which cannily with the canals arrange
a secret commerce so the sea may rise
in them and ebb and change?

Who sees me once is envious of my hound,
on which betimes in a distrait caress
my hand (which never charred to any passion),

invulnerable and richly jeweled, rests.
And noble youths, the hopes of ancient houses,
are ruined on my mouth, as if by poison.

DIE TREPPE DER ORANGERIE
VERSAILLES

Wie Könige, die schließlich nur noch schreiten
fast ohne Ziel, nur um von Zeit zu Zeit
sich den Verneigenden auf beiden Seiten
zu zeigen in des Mantels Einsamkeit—:

so steigt, allein zwischen den Balustraden,
die sich verneigen schon seit Anbeginn,
die Treppe: langsam und von Gottes Gnaden
und auf den Himmel zu und nirgends hin;

als ob sie allen Folgenden befahl
zurückzubleiben,—so daß sie nicht wagen,
von ferne nachzugehen; nicht einmal
die schwere Schleppe durfte einer tragen.

THE STEPS OF THE ORANGERY
VERSAILLES

LIKE worn-out kings who finally slowly stride
without a purpose, only now and then
to show the bowing suite on either side
the loneliness within the mantle's hem:

even so the steps between the balustrades,
which from the very first bowed to the stairs,
climb slowly, also by the grace of God,
toward the sky and lead not anywhere;

as though they had commanded all their horde
to stay far back and not approach again,
even so softly they could not be heard,
nor even dare to bear the heavy train.

DAS KARUSSELL

JARDIN DU LUXEMBOURG

Mit einem Dach und seinem Schatten dreht
sich eine kleine Weile der Bestand
von bunten Pferden, alle aus dem Land,
das lange zögert, eh es untergeht.
Zwar manche sind an Wagen angespannt,
doch alle haben Mut in ihren Mienen;
ein böser roter Löwe geht mit ihnen
und dann und wann ein weißer Elefant.

Sogar ein Hirsch ist da ganz wie im Wald,
nur daß er einen Sattel trägt und drüber
ein kleines blaues Mädchen aufgeschnallt.

Und auf dem Löwen reitet weiß ein Junge
und hält sich mit der kleinen heißen Hand,
dieweil der Löwe Zähne zeigt und Zunge.

Und dann und wann ein weißer Elefant.

Und auf den Pferden kommen sie vorüber,
auch Mädchen, helle, diesem Pferdesprunge
fast schon entwachsen; mitten in dem Schwunge
schauen sie auf, irgendwohin, herüber—

Und dann und wann ein weißer Elefant.

(Continued on page 84)

THE MERRY-GO-ROUND
JARDIN DU LUXEMBOURG

UNDER the roof and the roof's shadow turns
this train of painted horses for a while
in this bright land that lingers
before it perishes. In what brave style
they prance—though some pull wagons.
And there burns
a wicked lion red with anger...
and now and then a big white elephant.

Even a stag runs here, as in the wood,
save that he bears a saddle where, upright,
a little girl in blue sits, buckled tight.

And on the lion whitely rides a young
boy who clings with little sweaty hands,
the while the lion shows his teeth and tongue.

And now and then a big white elephant.

And on the horses swiftly going by
are shining girls who have outgrown this play;
in the middle of the flight they let their eyes
glance here and there and near and far away—

and now and then a big white elephant.

(Continued on page 85)

DAS KARUSSELL—*Continued*

Und das geht hin und eilt sich, daß es endet,
und kreist und dreht sich nur und hat kein Ziel.
Ein Rot, ein Grün, ein Grau vorbeigesendet,
ein kleines kaum begonnenes Profil.
Und manchesmal ein Lächeln, hergewendet,
ein seliges, das blendet und verschwendet
an dieses atemlose blinde Spiel.

THE MERRY-GO-ROUND—*Continued*

And all this hurries toward the end, so fast,
whirling futilely, evermore the same.
A flash of red, of green, of gray, goes past,
and then a little scarce-begun profile.
And oftentimes a blissful dazzling smile
vanishes in this blind and breathless game.

SPANISCHE TÄNZERIN

Wie in der Hand ein Schwefelzündholz, weiß,
eh es zur Flamme kommt, nach allen Seiten
zuckende Zungen streckt—: beginnt im Kreis
naher Beschauer hastig, hell und heiß
ihr runder Tanz sich zuckend auszubreiten.

Und plötzlich ist er Flamme ganz und gar.

Mit ihrem Blick entzündet sie ihr Haar
und dreht auf einmal mit gewagter Kunst
ihr ganzes Kleid in diese Feuersbrunst,
aus welcher sich, wie Schlangen, die erschrecken,
die nackten Arme wach und klappernd strecken.

Und dann: als würde ihr das Feuer knapp,
nimmt sie es ganz zusamm und wirft es ab
sehr herrisch, mit hochmütiger Gebärde
und schaut: da liegt es rasend auf der Erde
und flammt noch immer und ergibt sich nicht—.
Doch sieghaft, sicher und mit einem süßen
grüßenden Lächeln hebt sie ihr Gesicht
und stampft es aus mit kleinen festen Füßen.

SPANISH DANCER

As in the hand a match glows, swiftly white
before it bursts in flame and to all sides
licks its quivering tongues: within the ring
of spectators her wheeling dance is bright,
nimble, and fervid, twitches and grows wide.

And suddenly is made of pure fire.

Now her glances kindle the dark hair;
she twirls the floating skirts with daring art
into a whirlwind of consuming flame,
from which her naked arms alertly strike,
clattering like fearful rattlesnakes.

Then, as the fire presses her too closely,
imperiously she clutches it and throws it
with haughty gestures to the floor and watches
it rage and leap with flames that will not die—
until, victorious, surely, with a sweet
greeting smile, and holding her head high,
she tramples it to death with small, firm feet.

From NEUE GEDICHTE: ANDERER TEIL

A MON GRAND AMI
AUGUSTE RODIN

,ARCHAÏSCHER TORSO APOLLOS

Wir kannten nicht sein unerhörtes Haupt,
darin die Augenäpfel reiften. Aber
sein Torso glüht noch wie ein Kandelaber,
in dem sein Schauen, nur zurückgeschraubt,

sich hält und glänzt. Sonst könnte nicht der Bug
der Brust dich blenden, und im leisen Drehen
der Lenden könnte nicht ein Lächeln gehen
zu jener Mitte, die die Zeugung trug.

Sonst stünde dieser Stein entstellt und kurz
unter der Schultern durchsichtigem Sturz
und flimmerte nicht so wie Raubtierfelle

und bräche nicht aus allen seinen Rändern
aus wie ein Stern: denn da ist keine Stelle,
die dich nicht sieht. Du mußt dein Leben ändern.

TORSO OF AN ARCHAIC APOLLO

NEVER will we know his fabulous head
where the eyes' apples slowly ripened. Yet
his torso glows: a candelabrum set
before his gaze which is pushed back and hid,

restrained and shining. Else the curving breast
could not thus blind you, nor through the soft turn
of the loins could this smile easily have passed
into the bright groins where the genitals burned.

Else stood this stone a fragment and defaced,
with lucent body from the shoulders falling,
too short, not gleaming like a lion's fell;

nor would this star have shaken the shackles off,
bursting with light, until there is no place
that does not see you. You must change your life.

LEDA

Als ihn der Gott in seiner Not betrat,
erschrak er fast, den Schwan so schön zu finden;
er ließ sich ganz verwirrt in ihm verschwinden.
Schon aber trug ihn sein Betrug zur Tat,

bevor er noch des unerprobten Seins
Gefühle prüfte. Und die Aufgetane
erkannte schon den Kommenden im Schwane
und wußte schon: er bat um eins,

das sie, verwirrt in ihrem Widerstand,
nicht mehr verbergen konnte. Er kam nieder,
und halsend durch die immer schwächre Hand

ließ sich der Gott in die Geliebte los.
Dann erst empfand er glücklich sein Gefieder
und wurde wirklich Schwan in ihrem Schoß.

LEDA

WHEN the god in his need advanced toward
the swan, its beauty left him nigh dismayed;
but, though perplexed, he vanished in the bird.
Already his deft trickery betrayed

it to the deed before he had yet proved
the untried creature's feelings. But *she* knew
already who was in the swan and moved
the outcome of the one thing she must do.

Struggling and confused, she knew not whither
to hide from him, nor how she could withstand ...
his neck slipped through her ever-weakening hands,

and in the belov'd he let his godhead leap.
Then he first felt delight in all his feathers
and verily became swan in her lap.

DER ALCHIMIST

Sᴇʟᴛsᴀᴍ verlächelnd schob der Laborant
den Kolben fort, der halbberuhigt rauchte.
Er wußte jetzt, was er noch brauchte,
damit der sehr erlauchte Gegenstand

da drin entstände. Zeiten brauchte er.
Jahrtausende für sich und diese Birne,
in der es brodelte; im Hirn Gestirne
und im Bewußtsein mindestens das Meer.

Das Ungeheuere, das er gewollt,
er ließ es los in dieser Nacht. Es kehrte
zurück zu Gott und in sein altes Maß;

er aber, lallend wie ein Trunkenbold,
lag über dem Geheimfach und begehrte
den Brocken Gold, den er besaß.

THE ALCHEMIST

Smiling derisively, the chemist thrust
the retort from him, cooling as it smoked.
He knew exactly then what agents must
be added if that thing for which he looked

should gloriously be formed. He needed years,
whole aeons, for himself and this glass pear
where the stuff bubbled; needed constellations
in brain, and in perception at least an ocean.

That notion he had coveted, that monster,
he let loose in the night, and it aspired
straightway to God, and in its ancient measure;

but like a drunk man babbling, almost mad,
he lay among his mysteries and desired
only this gold crumb he already had.

DIE IRREN

Und sie schweigen, weil die Scheidewände
weggenommen sind aus ihrem Sinn,
und die Stunden, da man sie verstände,
heben an und gehen hin.

Nächtens oft, wenn sie ans Fenster treten:
plötzlich ist es alles gut.
Ihre Hände liegen im Konkreten,
und das Herz ist hoch und könnte beten,
und die Augen schauen ausgeruht

auf den unverhofften, oftentstellten
Garten im beruhigten Geviert,
der im Widerschein der fremden Welten
weiterwächst und niemals sich verliert.

THE INSANE

THEY are silent because the division walls
are broken down in the brain,
and hours when they might be understood at all
begin and leave again.

Often when they go to the window at night,
suddenly everything seems right:
their hands touch something tangible,
the heart is high and can pray,
the calmed eyes gaze

down on this unhoped-for, oft-distorted
garden in this peaceful square at rest,
which in the reflex of this foreign world
grows ever larger, never to be lost.

EINE VON DEN ALTEN

PARIS

ABENDS manchmal (weißt du, wie das tut?)
wenn sie plötzlich stehn und rückwärts nicken
und ein Lächeln, wie aus lauter Flicken,
zeigen unter ihrem halben Hut.

Neben ihnen ist dann ein Gebäude,
endlos, und sie locken dich entlang
mit dem Rätsel ihrer Räude,
mit dem Hut, dem Umhang und dem Gang.

Mit der Hand, die hinten unterm Kragen
heimlich wartet und verlangt nach dir:
wie um deine Hände einzuschlagen
in ein aufgehobenes Papier.

ONE OF THE OLD ONES

PARIS

OFTEN in the evening (you know what?)
she suddenly stands still, beckoning and watching,
and a smile, completely patches,
is shot at you from under the little hat.

Behind her are the buildings in a block
interminable, down which she coaxes
with the enigma of the scabby itch,
with the hat, the cape, and the slow walk.

With the hand behind the collar's nape,
waiting secretly and craving you:
as if to wrap your hand
in a picked-up piece of paper.

EINE WELKE

LEICHT, wie nach ihrem Tode
trägt sie die Handschuh, das Tuch.
Ein Duft aus ihrer Kommode
verdrängte den lieben Geruch,

an dem sie sich früher erkannte.
Jetzt fragte sie lange nicht, wer
sie sei (: eine ferne Verwandte),
und geht in Gedanken umher

und sorgt für ein ängstliches Zimmer,
das sie ordnet und schont,
weil es vielleicht noch immer
dasselbe Mädchen bewohnt.

FADED

Lightly, as after her death,
she carries the kerchief and gloves.
A perfume from her dressing-table
supplants the fragrance she loves,

by which she once knew herself.
Now she no longer asks
(this distant old relative)
who she is, but goes through her tasks,

anxiously tidies the room
with a prim old-maidish air,
because, perhaps, the same
girl is yet living there.

RÖMISCHE CAMPAGNA

Aus der vollgestellten Stadt, die lieber
schliefe, träumend von den hohen Thermen,
geht der grade Gräberweg ins Fieber;
und die Fenster in den letzten Fermen

sehn ihm nach mit einem bösen Blick.
Und er hat sie immer im Genick,
wenn er hingeht, rechts und links zerstörend,
bis er draußen atemlos beschwörend

seine Leere zu den Himmeln hebt,
hastig um sich schauend, ob ihn keine
Fenster treffen. Während er den weiten

Aquädukten zuwinkt herzuschreiten,
geben ihm die Himmel für die seine
ihre Leere, die ihn überlebt.

ROMAN CAMPAGNA

Out of the cluttered city which would rather
doze, dreaming of the lofty thermal springs,
smoothly the road of tombs descends in fever;
from the last farm the windows' glittering

follows the roadway with an evil look.
And the road has them always at his neck
as he goes down, destroying right and left,
till breathlessly, imploringly, he lifts

his very emptiness toward the sky,
glancing about him quickly, on the sly,
to see if any window still is spying.

And while he beckons the broad aqueducts
to come, the skies return as usufruct
for his small emptiness theirs which survive him.

DIE PARKE

I

Unaufhaltsam heben sich die Parke
aus dem sanft zerfallenden Vergehn;
überhäuft mit Himmeln, überstarke
Überlieferte, die überstehn,

um sich auf den klaren Rasenplänen
auszubreiten und zurückzuziehn,
immer mit demselben souveränen
Aufwand, wie beschützt durch ihn,

und den unerschöpflichen Erlös
königlicher Größe noch vermehrend,
aus sich steigend, in sich wiederkehrend:
huldvoll, prunkend, purpurn und pompös.

VII

Aber Schalen sind, drin der Najaden
Spiegelbilder, die sie nicht mehr baden,
wie ertrunken liegen, sehr verzerrt;
die Alleen sind durch Balustraden
in der Ferne wie versperrt.

Immer geht ein feuchter Blätterfall
durch die Luft hinunter wie auf Stufen,
jeder Vogelruf ist wie verrufen,
wie vergiftet jede Nachtigall.

(Continued on page 106)

THE PARKS

I

IRRESISTIBLY the parks arise
out of the easy crumbling of decay;
although weighed down by the enormous sky,
strong with tradition, they remain always

ready through the grassy pleasure-fields
to broaden out or quietly retire,
by this imperial spectacular
display which shields them

increasing still these inexhaustible earnings
of kingly greatness, growing more capacious,
mounting from themselves and there returning:
gracious, stately, purple, ostentatious.

VII

BUT there are shells in which the Naiads'
reflections bathe no more, but seem to lie
drowned on the bottom, changed and pulled awry;
and in the distance the stone balustrades
have closed the paths, as if with barricades.

And always now the moist leaves fall and fall
through the air, like running down the scale;
as if it were accursed is each bird's call,
and as if poisoned every nightingale.

(Continued on page 107)

DIE PARKE—*Continued*

Selbst der Frühling ist da nicht mehr gebend,
diese Büsche glauben nicht an ihn;
ungern duftet trübe, überlebend
abgestandener Jasmin

alt und mit Zerfallendem vermischt.
Mit dir weiter rückt ein Bündel Mücken,
so als würde hinter deinem Rücken
alles gleich vernichtet und verwischt.

THE PARKS—*Continued*

Spring itself has nothing more to give;
these bushes can no more believe in him;
unwillingly the gloomy, half-surviving
jasmine vine emits a frail perfume,

old and mixed with ruin. And a black
swarm of gnats is buzzing all about,
as if there, instantly! behind your back
everything were destroyed and blotted out.

DIE LAUTE

Ich bin die Laute. Willst du meinen Leib
beschreiben, seine schön gewölbten Streifen:
sprich so, als sprächest du von einer reifen
gewölbten Feige. Übertreib

das Dunkel, das du in mir siehst. Es war
Tullias Dunkelheit. In ihrer Scham
war nicht so viel, und ihr erhelltes Haar
war wie ein heller Saal. Zuweilen nahm

sie etwas Klang von meiner Oberfläche
in ihr Gesicht und sang zu mir.
Dann spannte ich mich gegen ihre Schwäche,
und endlich war mein Inneres in ihr.

THE LUTE

I am the lute, and if you wish to write
about my body with the lovely stripes
arching it, you must speak as of a ripe
full fig. You must exaggerate

the darkness that you see in me. It was
Tullia's darkness. In her shame
was not so much, and her bright gleaming hair
was like a shining hall. From time to time

she took the sound, reflected in her face,
and sang it back to me.
Then I grew taut toward her frailty,
until at last my being was in her.

DON JUANS KINDHEIT

Iɴ seiner Schlankheit war, schon fast entscheidend,
der Bogen, der an Frauen nicht zerbricht;
und manchmal, seine Stirne nicht mehr meidend,
ging eine Neigung durch sein Angesicht

zu einer, die vorüberkam, zu einer,
die ihm ein fremdes altes Bild verschloß:
er lächelte. Er war nicht mehr der Weiner,
der sich ins Dunkel trug und sich vergoß.

Und während ein ganz neues Selbstvertrauen
ihn öfter tröstete und fast verzog,
ertrug er ernst den ganzen Blick der Frauen,
der ihn bewunderte und ihn bewog.

DON JUAN'S CHILDHOOD

In his slim body was the implicit bow
already, that the women could not break;
and often, not avoiding now his brow,
upon his face an inclination woke

for this one going past, for that who kept
an ancient foreign portrait in her face;
he smiled. He was no more the boy who wept,
hiding himself away in a dark place.

And while a wholly new reliance rose
to solace him or warp his soul in turn,
gravely he bore the full strength of their gaze
which marveled at him and left him strangely torn.

DAME AUF EINEM BALKON

PLÖTZLICH tritt sie, in den Wind gehüllt,
licht in Lichtes, wie herausgegriffen,
während jetzt die Stube wie geschliffen
hinter ihr die Türe füllt

dunkel wie der Grund einer Kamee,
die ein Schimmern durchläßt durch die Ränder;
und du meinst, der Abend war nicht, ehe
sie heraustrat, um auf das Geländer

noch ein wenig von sich fortzulegen,
noch die Hände,—um ganz leicht zu sein:
wie dem Himmel von den Häuserreihn
hingereicht, von allem zu bewegen.

LADY ON A BALCONY

SWIFTLY she comes forth, wrapped in the wind,
bright in the light, as though she were snatched out,
while the black room seems cut
to fill the door behind her,

even as a cameo's dark background lets
a shimmering something softly through the edge;
you think: the evening was not here and light
until she came and leaned above the ledge,

putting for just a moment even her hands
away from her—that she might be aloof,
and turning them upward to the sky beyond
the dark row of the roofs.

ÜBUNG AM KLAVIER

DER Sommer summt. Der Nachmittag macht müde;
sie atmete verwirrt ihr frisches Kleid
und legte in die triftige Etüde
die Ungeduld nach einer Wirklichkeit,

die kommen konnte morgen, heute abend,
die vielleicht da war, die man nur verbarg;
und vor den Fenstern, hoch und alles habend,
empfand sie plötzlich den verwöhnten Park.

Da brach sie ab; schaute hinaus, verschränkte
die Hände, wünschte sich ein langes Buch
und schob auf einmal den Jasmingeruch
erzürnt zurück. Sie fand, daß er sie kränkte.

PIANO PRACTICE

Summer buzzes through the drowsy mood
of afternoon. Confused, she fluffs her fresh
dress, and into the profound étude
she plays impatiently a fretfulness

for something real that might befall tomorrow,
this evening, or perhaps now in the dark
is hidden. Suddenly through the lofty window
she is aware of the richly pampered park.

She breaks off playing, looks out, twines her hands,
wishes for some long book, and then, disturbed,
she pushes back the jasmine scent. She finds
the fragrance hurts.

DIE FLAMINGOS
PARIS, JARDIN DES PLANTES

In Spiegelbildern wie von Fragonard
ist doch von ihrem Weiß und ihrer Röte
nicht mehr gegeben, als dir einer böte,
wenn er von seiner Freundin sagt: sie war

noch sanft von Schlaf. Denn steigen sie ins Grüne
und stehn, auf rosa Stielen leicht gedreht,
beisammen, blühend, wie in einem Beet,
verführen sie verführender als Phryne

sich selber; bis sie ihres Auges Bleiche
hinhalsend bergen in der eignen Weiche,
in welcher Schwarz und Fruchtrot sich versteckt.

Auf einmal kreischt ein Neid durch die Volière;
sie aber haben sich erstaunt gestreckt
und schreiten einzeln ins Imaginäre.

THE FLAMINGOS
PARIS, JARDIN DES PLANTES

LIKE mirrored images by Fragonard,
so little of their red and white is shown,
and delicately, as if one came alone
and whispered of his mistress in your ear:

She lay there, flushed with sleep. . . . Above the green
reeds they rise and on their rose-stilts turn,
blooming together, as if on a parterre,
seducing (more seductively than Phryne)

themselves; and in the softness where the black
and apple-red are veiled they sink their necks,
hiding the pallid circles of their eyes,

till through their wire cage swift envy shrieks;
they waken in astonishment and stretch
themselves and soar imaginary skies.

DER EINSAME

NEIN: ein Turm soll sein aus meinem Herzen
und ich selbst an seinen Rand gestellt:
wo sonst nichts mehr ist, noch einmal Schmerzen
und Unsäglichkeit, noch einmal Welt.

Noch ein Ding allein im Übergroßen,
welches dunkel wird und wieder licht,
noch ein letztes, sehnendes Gesicht,
in das Nie-zu-Stillende verstoßen,

noch ein äußerstes Gesicht aus Stein,
willig seinen inneren Gewichten,
das die Weiten, die es still vernichten,
zwingen, immer seliger zu sein.

THE SOLITARY

No! a tower shall arise from my heart,
and I be placed at the top
where nothing else is, neither one last hurt,
nor the ineffable, where the world shall stop;

where there is nothing alone in the excess
to darken first and then again grow light;
nor even one last yearning face
banished in the not-to-be-silenced night;

nor even an uttermost one face of stone
yielding up the center of its weight,
so that the distance that annihilates it
shall force it to a yet more blessèd fate.

DAS KIND

Unwillkürlich sehn sie seinem Spiel
lange zu; zuweilen tritt das runde
seiende Gesicht aus dem Profil,
klar und ganz wie eine volle Stunde,

welche anhebt und zu Ende schlägt.
Doch die andern zählen nicht die Schläge,
trüb von Mühsal und vom Leben träge;
und sie merken gar nicht, wie es trägt—,

wie es alles trägt, auch dann, noch immer,
wenn es müde in dem kleinen Kleid
neben ihnen wie im Wartezimmer
sitzt und warten will auf seine Zeit.

THE CHILD

WITHOUT intending it, they watch his play
a long while, and sometimes a living round
face turns from the profile and straightway
is clear and full: an hour about to sound

completion with uplifted blow. But these
do not count the strokes; they are too worn
with misery and tired from life to see
the child and all that his slight life has borne,

and how he bears it now and must bear yet,
when near to them, as in a waiting-room,
wearily in his little dress he sits,
until his time shall come.

DER KÄFERSTEIN

SIND nicht Sterne fast in deiner Nähe,
und was gibt es, das du nicht umspannst,
da du dieser harten Skarabäe
Karneolkern gar nicht fassen kannst

ohne jenen Raum, der ihre Schilder
niederhält, auf deinem ganzen Blut
mitzutragen; niemals war er milder,
näher, hingegebener. Er ruht

seit Jahrtausenden auf diesen Käfern,
wo ihn keiner braucht und unterbricht;
und die Käfer schließen sich und schläfern
unter seinem wiegenden Gewicht.

THE SCARAB

Are not the constellations here already?
What is there that you do not enfold
now, since you cannot hold
this hard carnelian-kernel scarab-body

without receiving within all your blood
this mighty space that weighs down the wing-shards?
Never was space milder, never shared
itself so, nor was nearer.

Thousands of years upon these beetles, deep
where none can use or hinder it, space waits;
the beetles shut themselves up, growing sleepy,
beneath its cradling weight.

BUDDHA IN DER GLORIE

MITTE aller Mitten, Kern der Kerne,
Mandel, die sich einschließt und versüßt,—
dieses alles bis an alle Sterne
ist dein Fruchtfleisch: Sei gegrüßt.

Sieh, du fühlst, wie nichts mehr an dir hängt;
im Unendlichen ist deine Schale,
und dort steht der starke Saft und drängt.
Und von außen hilft ihm ein Gestrahle,

denn ganz oben werden deine Sonnen
voll und glühend umgedreht.
Doch in dir ist schon begonnen,
was die Sonnen übersteht.

THE BUDDHA IN THE GLORY

CENTER of centers, of all seeds the germ,
O almond self-enclosed and growing sweeter,
from here clear to the starry swarms
your fruit's flesh grows. I greet you.

Lo, you feel how nothing more depends
on you; into infinity your shell
waxes; there the strong sap works and fills you.
And from beyond a gloriole descends

to help, for high above your head your suns,
full and fulgurating, turn.
And yet, already in you is begun
something which longer than the suns shall burn.

NOTES

DAS BUCH DER BILDER

Pages 18–19, Initiation—

One is let immediately into Rilke's secret of making his reader participate in the re-creation of a poem. As a spider spins the web from her own body, the poet erects the dark tree against the sky and makes his world. (Cf. Schopenhauer's "the world is my representation.") Here are the same weary eyes as in other poems—eyes weary of common sights, of books,—but it is with the eyes of the mind that the more real world of the seer is observed.

Pages 20–21, The Knight—

This macabre image of Death squatting within the armor would have delighted Holbein. The same idea occurs several times in *Die Aufzeichnungen des Malte Laurids Brigge:* "Meinem Großvater noch, dem alten Kammerherrn Brigge, sah man es an, daß er einen Tod in sich trug" (p. 14); "Sie alle haben einen eignen Tod gehabt. Diese Männer, die ihn in der Rüstung trugen . . ." (pp. 21–22). The death of the old Chamberlain is one of the best parts of the book.

Pages 22–23, Madness—

This girl is as mad as Ophelia, as Lear, or a hatter, but the illusion of grandeur typical of her case makes her rather happier about it than the inmates of the asylum who have lucid moments and are then lost again in "this oft-distorted garden" (see "The Insane," p. 97). Here is the Nietzschean Dionysiac gay madness rather than the Biblical type of possession by a demon.

Pages 24–25, The Angels—

These pathetic, anemic, epicene angels, with yellow water-waved hair and long white robes, these angels all alike, as they are to be found in the paintings of the Primitives, in Blake's drawings, or in the church windows designed by Burne-Jones, are not particularly impressive. One likes the seldom used irony of the poet in recording their yearning for parenthetic sin. The poem seems to me important because Rilke is describing the "broad sculptor-hands" of Rodin.

And it's a grand simile that relates the mighty rush of the angels' wings to God's turning through the vast pages of the dark book of the Beginning. But these angels have merely the importance of rests in music.

Pages 26-27, From a Childhood—

Compare this memory of his mother with the *Malte* (p. 117): "... Maman kam herein in der großen Hofrobe, die sie gar nicht in acht nahm, und lief beinah und ließ ihren weißen Pelz hinter sich fallen und nahm mich in die bloßen Arme. Und ich befühlte, erstaunt und entzückt wie nie, ihr Haar und ihr kleines, gepflegtes Gesicht und die kalten Steine an ihren Ohren und die Seide am Rand ihrer Schultern, die nach Blumen dufteten." There is great love in this poem, intensified perhaps by the mother's casual and litotic "Are you here?"—as if she hadn't known all along that the shy boy would be there, waiting for what seems almost a secret love-tryst. And there is much wistfulness and suffering in the last stanza as the great-eyed boy watches the tired bejeweled hands on the white keys. See also the other poems on music, "The Last Evening" (p. 77) and "Piano Practice" (p. 115).

Pages 28-29, The Neighbor—

This is the outcry of an exile who feels himself pursued, almost "picked on," by the music of an equally lonely man. Cf. "Ich sitze hier in meiner kleinen Stube ... Ich sitze hier und bin nichts ... fünf Treppen hoch, an einem grauen Pariser Nachmittag .." *Malte* (p. 29). "The heaviness of things [*Dinge*]" is one of his major themes. This poem gains in the original by the proximity of "Menschen bei Nacht" and the blind man in "Pont du Carrousel," two profoundly lonely poems.

Pages 30-31, The Solitary—

This belongs to the same group. Rilke had made several journeys to foreign lands: Italy, in 1897, 1903, 1904; Russia, in 1899. Later travels included Sweden, in 1905, and Egypt, in 1910. My point is that the solitary traveler is just the man who would be most exposed to the museums, galleries, cathedrals, city squares, and so forth, which Rilke describes in so many poems. He has eaten his bread in tears and is not unaware of the powers of heaven. One almost sees the "full days" like wooden mugs of beer on Swedish tables, contrasted with the inner life of the poet to whom only the far-away is filled with realities, which I take to be implied by "Figur." The whole poem is a fine example of the *Zwiespalt,* the dichotomy which Rilke, like other poets, felt in his relation to ordinary life.

Pages 32–33, Lament—

In a similar mood of perplexity about the world, he turns to the stars with the same assurance as did Ptolemy (in the *Greek Anthology*), Dante at the ends of the three parts of the *Comedy,* and the serene philosopher of Königsberg. This is one of a group of poems (from which I have done six) which reveal his misfitness for life and his ingrained melancholy.

Pages 34–35, Solitude—

After its topic sentence, this piece works principally with rain and its effect on people in the gray hour of dawn; but the identity of rain with solitude is finally established in the splendidly isolated last line, itself a mute symbol of loneliness. At the beginning of the nineteenth century, the Romantics in all countries wrote about their individual solitude. Rilke makes it universal: Everyman's loneliness, even, or especially, in the city. For contrast, compare Shelley's "Euganean Hills" and the many rather futile and wishy-washy poems of *Waldeinsamkeit* from the Germans.

Pages 36–37, Autumn Day—

Not so lush and vivid as its famous companion piece by Keats. When the latter wrote his "Ode to Autumn," he was a man about to die, toying with a gentle melancholy induced by his disease. When Rilke wrote this, he was a man condemned to live, not in a poetic water-color dabbling at existence, but in the deep and irrevocable burin strokes on the copper-plate of reality. This is autumn with its fullness and fruitfulness contrasted with the thin husks which the poet was stuffing in his mental belly during this period. Many times the prophecies in the last stanza have smitten me on the nose of stoical fortitude, yet left me undismayed, and primarily because there is a strong ringing overtone which sounds in the reader's ear: "He overcame this; you shall, also!" Nor is this piece so carelessly devastating as Verlaine's "Chanson d'Automne." Rilke speaks to a larger audience; Verlaine's poem is the wailing of a spanked child, of a self-commiserating weakling.

Pages 38–39, Memory—

Since autumn is the season of revery, it is proper that one of the series should be set in a library. He is a man—you—brooding in the last glow of sunset, waiting for something to happen. He remembers the foreign countries he has traveled in, the women, their garments, the art galleries. Then, suddenly, as most of his visions are introduced, the lost and irrevocable year stands before him. Poe said that "Nevermore" was the saddest word in the language, and himself used it memorably.

Pages 40–41, End of Autumn—

An example of the poet's metrical resources. Line 1 in the German has three long *i* sounds. There are several *t*'s in the first stanza. Line 5 has three *al* rhymes; and four *g*'s are heard in the second stanza. Notice the *gilbenden* and *gelben* rhymes. In line 9 are four initial *w*'s and six hard monosyllables, three ending in a vowel and *r*. That's hard to beat.

Pages 42–43, Autumn—

A consoling assurance that the apparent destruction of things is but part of the eternal order. It all happens in the hands of God: those "broad sculptor-hands." One is reminded here of a Buddhist story in which Hannuman, the monkey son of the wind god in the Hindu pantheon, wagers the Buddha that he can leap out of sight. He takes a deep breath and makes a mighty spring. Returning, he tells the Buddha of five gigantic red sandstone pillars which he has seen and marked at the very outer rim of space. Quietly Sakyamuni shows the Haliburton monkey his hand, with little scratches on the fingers, and asks, "Did they look anything like these?" The story is better than the poem.

Pages 44–45, Evening—

Evening is akin to autumn. In stanza 3 the reader again feels himself in the situation presented in "Autumn Day" (p. 36), but here is a typical Rilkean chance to amalgamate oneself with the symbols of stone for the earth and stars for the sky: a cosmic unity in place of the confusion and fear of human existence.

Pages 46–49, Solemn Hour and Strophes—

These poems link directly with "Autumn" (p. 42). We are in God's hand—and this is a stimulation from the statue of that name by Rodin; but here we find a pantheistic suggestion of God, not only "in the mind of man," but in his very blood, which seems more warmly intimate than the purely cerebral occupation by deity of a nasty pinkish sponge with dubious thinking powers.

Pages 50–51, The Song of the Waif—

I have skipped a section of long poems which are not particularly noteworthy, to an example from "Voices," a group which includes songs from earth's disinherited: the beggar, the blind man, the drunkard, the suicide, the widow, the idiot, the orphan, the dwarf, and the leper. Who can beat this Homeric catalogue of life's unfortunates? This is an erratic piece of rhyming, but the plangent note of desolation is comparable to that in Theodor Storm's "Waisenkind," which is quotably succinct:

> Ich bin eine Rose, pflück mich geschwind!
> Blos liegen die Würzlein dem Regen und Wind.
>
> Nein, geh nur vorüber und lass du mich los!
> Ich bin keine Blume, ich bin keine Ros'.
>
> Wohl wehet mein Röcklein, wohl fasst mich der Wind;
> Ich bin nur ein vater- und mutterlos Kind.

The lock of the mother's hair in Rilke's poem, the sole relic of either parent after the father's death, is particularly affecting. Here one sees the hopeless desolation of the poor—one is tempted to say, of those on the alphabetical dole system. See how much more moving Rilke's is than Storm's, which gets off into a sort of sweet pathos, like that of Dickens.

Pages 52–53, From a Stormy Night [VI and VIII]—

Olivero (p. 142 of his book) has suavely anticipated me by calling this series "an album of nine etchings."

The book concludes with a short drama between Death and a blind man, and "Requiem," which is dedicated to his wife.

NEUE GEDICHTE: ERSTER TEIL

In this book Rilke achieves a perfect mastery of form, especially in the sonnets and twelve-liners. His essay on Rodin should be read in connection with many of the poems.

Pages 56–57, Early Apollo—

When one remembers the expressionless, not to say dumb, faces of early Greek sculpture, he is surprised that such a prophecy can be evoked from the unanimated features of the god. But here it is: a perfect little history of the development of the Greek lyric after Apollo awakens and becomes, in addition to being a solar deity, a culture god, the god of song. One recognizes again the poet's favorite rose petals. In the original, *g*'s and *k*'s give coherence to the octave; the sestet is tightened by several *b*'s.

Pages 58–59, Oblation—

This links the poet's cult of childhood with a delicate troubadour love and the symbols of Christian worship. The glistening of water is a motif to be found repeatedly in his later verse.

Pages 60–61, The Buddha—

The first of three poems on this subject. I have used two. This poem, much lower in key than the one he chose for the last of his book (p. 125), was written in Paris in 1905. (Cf. *Briefe,* 1902–1906, pp. 262 ff., 274 f., 290, 321.) According to a note given me by Frau Ruth Sieber-Rilke, her mother remembers that this poem is about a statue in Rodin's garden at Meudon. (Cf. *Gesammelte Werke,* IV, 408.) I made a futile pilgrimage there; the garden had been stripped. In the Rodin Museum in Paris the statue had lost its importance because of comparison with the many others.

Pages 62–63, The Panther—

Perhaps the best of his several poems on animals in captivity. Line 3 is typical of his capricious versification: "Stäbe gäbe," which I have feebly reproduced. Line 9 refers to the nictitating membrane.

Pages 64–65, The Gazelle—

See the Introduction for a full discussion. This seems to me to be one of the key poems for understanding his technique.

Pages 66–67, Roman Sarcophagi—

This, another museum piece, shows his interest in carved stone, his desire to connect even dead matter with life, and his use of water as a symbol of the enduring essence of the world. (Cf. pp. 59, 103, above, and *Die Sonette an Orpheus,* Pt. I, x.)

Pages 68–69, The Swan—

A fine example of his symbolism. The swan represents both life and death. As he enters the water, we are put under the spell of a truly Rilkean moment: the entrance of an awkward being into that mystery in which it not only becomes more beautiful, but in which its forward movement seems to be the mature fulfillment of the meaning of life. I have reproduced in line 6 his own purposely clumsy phrase to represent this transition.

Pages 70–71, A Woman's Fate—

This speaks for itself: a splendid understanding of what can happen to women. It is infinitely tender, universal, but not at all sentimental. The carelessness of the king, the fragility of glass, the cupboard where a shelved thing has no real existence, make this poem one of his happiest analogies.

Pages 72–73, Blue Hydrangeas—

This haunted me for several years before I could tackle it. The very deftness with which the poet presents a new understanding of flowers at the end of autumn (despite the use of pathetic fallacy, toward which one feels that even Ruskin would this time have turned a benign eye) makes this a tour de force and a minor masterpiece. Just imagine how solemnly Wordsworth or Bryant would have treated the subject. Line 1 refers to the darkest green of the painter's gamut, a dab of rough, dried paint. The apron was probably one of his daughter's. This seems to me to be the best of several poems on flowers in the book.

Pages 74–75, Before the Summer Rain—

An indication of his interest in parks and childhood. Notice the darkness and melancholy with which he invests even the living rain. And the bird's reminding him of the saint is priceless. In the sestet he uses the future, the present, and the past tense in his verbs and somehow achieves an effect of time's having been reversed in its motion until it leads one back into memories of childhood. In *Malte* (pp. 153 ff.) he does some fine interpretations of the six tapestries of "La Dame à la Licorne" in the Musée de Cluny. The poem will receive considerable emotional glow if the faded red and cobalt blue of these tapestries are remembered.

Pages 76–77, The Last Evening—

Inscribed in the guest book of Frau Nonna (Baroness Julie von Nordeck zur Rabenau) in Capri, March 18, 1907. (Cf. *Briefe*, 1907–1914, p. 80.) This is one of Rilke's most delicately conceived studies in the differing attitudes of the sexes toward a given situation. The male egoist sees himself in the woman's face and feels that he's doing rather a fine job of impressing her with his sorrow. She is undergoing the more real suffering. The poem gains in power by its final concentration, not on the people concerned, but on the shako as a symbol. This black fur contraption with the startling white skull was the badge of one of Germany's crack regiments. Only Rilke would have thought to show it on a mirror-topped table, doubling the ominous sign and making death seem twice certain. Compare this man's face with that of the monk playing the organ in Giorgione's "Concert."

Pages 78–79, The Courtesan—

In Part Two of the *Neue Gedichte* are five other poems about Venice. I do not feel that the present piece was necessarily done there. I looked in vain for a possible original for the study. In the Correr Museum in Venice, Carpaccio's "Courtesans" may have served him. The color of the hair, the jeweled hands stroking the dog, the slender brows, are there; but the women look so stupid that it's impossible to imagine either of them indulging in a little dramatic monologue about herself. The comparison of the eyebrows with the bridges, the "commerce" between her eyes and the sea which is the life-blood of the city, are other organic figures growing from the very stuff of the subject—as if a sculptor pinched a lump of clay from part of his modeling and applied it to another place: it's all of a piece. And "commerce" has to me, at least, something of a play on words. The octave of this sonnet rhymes *a bbb a ccc* and runs over into the sestet in the original. Burckhardt in his *Renaissance* has an interesting section on this part of Venetian life.

Pages 80–81, The Steps of the Orangery—

The Orangery lies between two great stairways called the *Cent Marches* (it somehow pleased me to find that they have 103 and 105 steps, respectively). The balustrades really seem very insignificant and the broad stairs very lonely. The force of line 8 can be felt only by standing below and looking up, as the poet of course did. Then one forgets the palace on the terrace, and the stairs lead to the sky. The play of thought here is admirably carried out: the lonely stairs and the aged king, the crumbling (bowing) balustrades and the nodding courtiers, and the king and stairs both climbing "by the grace of God." There are thirteen long *i*'s in the first six lines of the original. Any other poet would have made a sonnet; Rilke knows when he is through.

Pages 82–83, The Merry-Go-Round—

This merry-go-round is still in use. It is a primitive contraption under a tent among the chestnut trees of the garden. The motive power is supplied by a hulk of a man who grinds a large wheel. Worst of all, there is no organ and the animals do not rise and fall on cams. But the children seem not to mind such minor defects. The names of the steeds are fascinating and determine the popularity of the mounts. The horses are painted with cheerful names: Bijou, Félix, Charlot, Papillon, Gamin, and Coco. Three, probably triplets, are called Loulou, Lolo, and Lulu. I suspect recent tampering in the names of Mickey, Donald, and Epinard. But children refuse to be bamboozled; I have never seen anyone on this last poor creature, named after the loveless vegetable. There is a giraffe called Fatima. The two stags, Rapide and Pied Léger, have dilapidated antlers mauled by hundreds of hands. The lions, black Brutus and red Sultan, are splendidly carnivorous, with fine great teeth and drooling tongues. The grand white elephants which seem so large in the poem and bob magically up and down are really two small, lovable, roly-poly calves called Rizi and Toby. Oh, yes, and there are two old, red, moth-eaten camels, Simoun and Siroco, whom the children will not ride for love or money—the humps refuse to conform to childish anatomy; the animals have an eternal hungry look, and seem to have perpetual snuffles. I have been past this place on dozens of autumn and winter afternoons, and there is always a crowd of children and a sprinkling of mothers grouped here. A brown ground-swirl of leaves serves for a carpet. The man who takes the tickets is very generous in helping the younger children to spear the brass rings which give free rides. An air of sweetness and naïveté pervades the place; a ride costs 50 centimes; I once rode one of the poor, lonely, old camels myself. The movement of the verse as the girls "glance here and there and near and far away" does something toward reproducing the easy bounding motion of the original. In at least two of the poet's letters he says that this poem was almost the only one which was sure of enthusiastic reception when he read it before an audience. I have been criticized for not rhyming the refrain. In German the last syllable carries the accent, but there's very little to be done with a dactylic word in English.

Pages 86–87, Spanish Dancer—

Rilke saw this dancer at the christening party of Zuloaga's daughter, Ruth Sieber-Rilke tells me. One is reminded of Sargent's "Carmencita," the dancer in the yellow dress. I have got the nine *k* sounds of the original in the second stanza. These prepare the reader for the unmentioned castanets. *Klappernd* and *Schlange* really combine to *Klapperschlange,* which is "rattlesnake."

NEUE GEDICHTE: ANDERER TEIL

Pages 90–91, Torso of an Archaic Apollo—

This is the second initial poem on this subject. It is Greek, but is seen through Rodin's eyes. The last poem in the book, which is on the Buddha, is a piece also inspired by a statue. It bears by implication the full weight of the last sentence of the present selection, "You must change your life." The brightness of the beauty of godhead is so strong and all-embracing that one can never escape it, but must change himself and his life to fit into the established plan. In the Archaic Room of the Louvre are three torsos of Apollo, but that from the Theater of Miletus, early fifth century, so overwhelms those from Actium and Paros that one is certain it is the subject of the poem. Nor do the two smaller statues fulfill exactly all the qualities described. The meaning of line 8 seems to my male advisers justly translated; there have been complaints from the more intuitive sex.

Pages 92–93, Leda—

The importance of this legend in art and literature warrants perhaps a fuller discussion of Rilke's use of it than space permits. It contains the germ of the Homeric poems and the later tragedies dealing with the heroes after the war. Of the many pictures and statues of this subject, one remembers the copy of the painting by Da Vinci which has disappeared—in which, with the typical simper of Da Vinci's women, Leda gazes at the earth where two broken shells have already released the four immortal cygnets, who sprawl among the flowers. Mother and the father-bird stand in much the posture of those photographs of our grandparents. But the emphasis, after all, is on the results of the union. Correggio takes the affair at high tide in his softest, most voluptuous style; the whole thing is fluffy and fuzzy, all flesh and feathers. Of the statues, one can hardly escape that in Florence by Ammannati, which is indebted to the female figures of the Medicean tombs—the Leda has a silly face and a muscular, stringy thigh; it is an unpleasant piece of work. The smaller figure in the Archaeological Museum at Venice is frankly bawdy and very amusing. But the presence of the story in one of the

details of the famous bronze Jubilee Doors of St. Peter's gives one
an unholy shock, and the brisk treatment of the event makes one
feel rather more kindly toward the frigid baroque barn behind the
doors. One wishes that Dante had put Leda in his seventh circle,
where she richly belonged for having violated nature. Now consider
how the story has fared in the literature of our time. In *Faust,* Part II,
lines 6903–6920, Homunculus relates the dream he is reading in
Faust's mind. There is a deal of life flame in the noble body, of
rustling, fluttering, and splashing, but the gentlemanly little mani-
kin draws a thick curtain of vapor over the finale as if the tableau
were being presented to a parlorful of *Backfische* in fluffy white
gowns with pink sashes. After all, Goethe is pretty much eighteenth
century. But may I present a line-for-line translation from a poem
on the subject from *Divertissements* by Rémy de Gourmont?

LEDA

The innocent Leda was bathing her naked limbs,
The grace of her body enchanted the river-water,
And the reeds of the marshes, seized with a strange agitation,
Were singing a song as old as it was new,

When the swan appeared, white ship upon the stream.

When the swan appeared, white ship with a golden prow,
Leda trembled with joy and stood there dreaming,
Then, slowly, without noise, she came to the bank
And lay down in the grass, in the shadow of an ilex;

The bird came nearer, beautiful, ardent, and dreaming.

The bird neared, beautiful, ardent, with an air
So regal and vigorous that Leda was charmed
And regretted in this illusion of her flesh
Not being a swan herself that she might be loved

Under the shadows, among the pleasant soft grasses.

In the shadows, among the soft grass and the lilies,
Leda gives way to the weight of this arrogant bird,
All dripping yet with the waters of Simoïs,
And her startled body, shivering, resigns itself

To caressing only the plumage of a swan.

Observe that the treatment here is lush, merely physiological, after the French manner. The reader is referred to this author's *Physique de l'Amour* for an explanation of the swan's peculiar fitness in this legend. For an example of a much more modern version, I am indebted to Count Brunetto of Agrigento: not only for his permission to use one of his unpublished poems, but also for his help in getting it into English of a sort one stormy day in his villa by the Mediterranean. The treatment here is modern, ironic, psychological, and even pathological.

ORNITHOLOGICAL IDYLL

The swan, for all his white pride, was obsessed
By more than April when the Olympian lecher
Hid in his body, stirring his bright breast
Perversely toward an unknown treachery.
Leda slid halfway in the green water,
But started from that intimate cold touch.
The bird swam boldly, sensing the shrewd matter
At hand, devising the unique attack.

And when she stroked his muscular neck and laid
Her breasts against his feathers for their heat,
She was a girl more curious than lewd,
Shuddering as she felt a god's pulse beat . . .
But clutched the bird to her and felt no fear—
As if she hugged a pillow in her sleep.
That innocent plumage! Ah, what epic fire
Leaped forth to spotlight this lame maiden-slip.

Notice that both these poets—and Yeats, too—put the emphasis on the woman and her reactions, whereas Rilke spends most of his lines on the bird. Isn't there a fundamental difference here, and is not Rilke's sensuous handling—if such it be—more akin to the manner of the Greeks, childlike and unashamed? I have gone into this perhaps at too great length because an understanding of his point of view seems worth the trouble.

Pages 94–95, The Alchemist—

(I have skipped a dozen Biblical poems here.) A few years ago gold was actually produced from base metals—and in Oregon, of all places! The "glass pear" is, of course, the retort. There is a bigness of the sweep of time in this, which is Rilke at his best: after the aeons, an ironic tapering off to the tiny crumb of gold.

Pages 96–97, The Insane—

A poetic interpretation of dissociation. The short fourth and fifth lines of the second stanza are typical iconoclasms. It would have made a better twelve-liner. (Cf. "Madness," p. 23.)

Pages 98–99, One of the Old Ones—

Let me quote from *Malte* (p. 248): "Diese Stadt ist voll von solche, die langsam zu ihnen hinabgleiten. Die meisten sträuben sich.erst; aber dann gibt es diese verbleichenden, alterenden Mädchen, die sich fortwährend ohne Widerstand hinüberlassen, starke, im Inneresten ungebrauchte, die nie geliebt worden sind." Typical of his interest in the underprivileged. (Cf. the next poem.)

Pages 100–101, Faded—

This is a tender and accurate study of an old maid who must now resort to artificial perfumes to replace the loss of her youthful blooming fragrance: a loss which is symbolical of the fading of her personality until she seems merely the old aunt of the girl she once was. I have observed this tragedy many times.

Pages 102–103, Roman Campagna—

In the second quatrain the sonnet form is violated; it consists of two sets of couplets. *Fermen* is a word made by Rilke from the French *ferme*. The poem is almost humorous in its conception of the personified road, fearful of the windows, yet doomed to have them always at his neck. Compare M.D. Herter Norton, *Letters to a Young Poet,* page 42, where it reads: "Waters unendingly full of life go over the old aqueducts . . . and dance in the many squares over white stone basins."

Pages 104–105, The Parks—

The poet is definitely interested in parks, for he had wandered in many and lived on the estates of various friends and patrons. Much of the material in the seven poems of this set was gathered from Versailles. He specifically mentions the *Tapis vert,* the smiling Dianas, the stairs and the Naiads, and he seems to have looked at these studies through the eyes of Watteau and Fragonard, for he uses their very tones: silver, rose, gray, white, and blue. The end of VII, where the swarm of gnats blots out the world behind one's back, is one of his grandest moments. It is as if Shiva the Destroyer were right behind one.

Pages 108–109, The Lute—

A museum piece. Tullia was probably any one of the gay young Venetian ladies of the Renaissance. The instrument is the ancestor of the mandolin. One can see the poet bending over a glass case and making notations for his poem. This is a twelve-liner with two four-foot verses inserted. It reminds one of Browning's "Dear dead women, and such hair too!" I wish I had never tackled this.

Pages 110–111, Don Juan's Childhood—

If one considers Baudelaire's Don Juan poem as a final exit piece for the great lover, this one might well serve to introduce the series of plays and poems on the subject. It's sad to think of this splendid boy growing up only to be crushed under vindictive marble.

Pages 112–113, Lady on a Balcony—

The figure of a bored or harassed woman, standing sharply in white against the cameo's background, the black doorway, is unforgettable. This is another twelve-liner with occasional short verses.

Pages 114–115, Piano Practice—

An aristocrat, unhappy, unmated, is yearning for the great adventure. She has had, perhaps, a touch of romance, which explains the hurt she gets from the jasmine's scent.

Pages 116–117, The Flamingos—

This is one of the supreme poems, in any language, about birds. It makes the swallow songs of the Greeks, Lesbia's sparrow, and the whole flock of English skylarks and nightingales look as if they were perpetually moulting. Even Byrant's waterfowl is a bit dimmed by comparison. And Wordsworth's bird—"Happy, happy liver!" The condition of the descendants or successors of these birds seems to me rather more cheerful than that described here. About a dozen of them—they deftly evaded census—live in a half-acre of grass with a pool. There is no *volière* in the sense that Rilke implies. They were going through a fairly orderly quadrille with not ungraceful gestures when I called. From time to time they flapped their wings and shrieked mightily, but they appeared to enjoy it and certainly made no effort to fly away. Perhaps they have grown accustomed to captivity; maybe they were born here and feel at home; or the highly amusing seal who shares the pool may keep them contented. I got none of the acute sense of pain from the actual experience that I do from the poem. Perhaps this is the true function of poetry: to make things absent work more powerfully than the reality.

Pages 118–119, The Solitary—

Not to be confused with an earlier poem of the same title. One has only to contrast the two poems to see how far on the *Via Dolorosa* the poet has come. Here he longs for something beyond the usual ivory tower of romantic escape. All this is in harmony with the motif of the last part of his book: loneliness, detachment, wistfulness for a place beyond mortal suffering, past the changes inherent in the universe, beyond even the white face of love. I have attempted to represent this in the poems chosen from his finale. It seems to end in a Buddhist annihilation or an absorption into something which might be called God. This poem has to be grown into and requires orientation in the sacred books of the East if the vague symbols are to be felt—they cannot be explained. It should be read in connection with the last poem. The individual is striving to pass out of space into something which is either nothingness or a divine whole.

Pages 120–121, The Child—

Perhaps nothing is more pathetic than this awakening in a child of the feeling of group consciousness. The elders make no effort to understand it and to feel themselves into its problems. The figure of life as a waiting room recalls "Memory" (p. 39). There is another profile in "The Merry-Go-Round" (p. 83). The figure of the hour about to sound suggests a clock's face which fits with the waiting room. In lines 5–9 of the original there are five rhymes in *-ägt,* a heavy syllable which seems to add to the child's burden. And here is a profound sense of time. Compare *Letters to a Young Poet,* pages 45–46: "To be solitary, the way one was solitary as a child, when the grown-ups went round entangled with things that seemed important and big because grown-ups looked so busy and because one comprehended nothing of their doings."

Pages 122–123, The Scarab—

This penultimate poem of the *Neue Gedichte* is another piece conceived in a museum; for as yet Rilke had not been in Egypt. But he has changed a casual experience into an important part of his book by linking the motifs of time and space and leading to his climax in the last poem. The little stone beetles become the symbol of a heavy and eternal vastness. Space, like an embodied postulate, rests on their wing shards.

Pages 124–125, The Buddha in the Glory—

Her mother's recollection, Ruth Sieber-Rilke tells me, was that "one of the Buddha poems was written about the great statue in the Völkerkunde Museum in Berlin. This must be the last poem, 'Buddha in der Glorie.'" In an early preparation for this poem (p. 61), the Buddha is shown as unaware of the presence of his worshipers. Here he is apotheosized; he becomes the center of all space and time. The figure of the self-enclosed, ever-ripening almond is daring but exact: the Buddha thus is made the seed of all existence. The shell is in infinity, and time is struck in a full final chord by "something more enduring than the suns."

BIBLIOGRAPHY

BIBLIOGRAPHY

Works of Rainer Maria Rilke Used in the Preparation of This Book

Das Buch der Bilder, in *Gesammelte Werke,* Band II, Leipzig, Insel-Verlag, 1927.
Neue Gedichte, in *Gesammelte Werke,* Band III, Leipzig, Insel-Verlag, 1927.
Die Aufzeichnungen des Malte Laurids Brigge, in *Gesammelte Werke,* Band V, Leipzig, Insel-Verlag, 1927.
Briefe aus den Jahren 1902 bis 1906, hrsg. von Ruth Sieber-Rilke und Carl Sieber, Leipzig, Insel-Verlag, 1930.

Books, Monographs, and Studies on Rilke

Baltusz, Mitsou. *Préface de Rainer Maria Rilke.* Erlenbach/Zürich u. Leipzig, Rotapfel-Verlag, 1921.
Bartels, A. *Die deutsche Dichtung von Hebbel bis zur Gegenwart.* Leipzig, Haessel, 1922.
Berendt, H. "Rainer Maria Rilke, zu den Aufzeichnungen des Malte Laurids Brigge," *Mitteilungen der Literarhistorischen Gesellschaft Bonn,* 6. Jahrgang, Heft 4, 1911.
Betz, Maurice. *Petite Stèle pour Rainer Maria Rilke.* Strassburg, Heissler, 1927.
Betz, Maurice. *Reconnaissance à (R. M.) Rilke.* Paris, Emile-Paul, 1927.
Bianquis, G. *La Poésie autrichienne de Hofmannsthal à Rilke.* Paris, Les Presses Universitaires de France, 1926.
Borkowsky, E., *Neue deutsche Lyrik vom Naturalismus bis zur Gegenwart.* Breslau, Hirt, 1925.
Buchheit, Gert. *Rainer Maria Rilke.* Zürich, Rascher, 1928.
Buchheit, Stefan. *Abschied von Rilke.* Tübingen, Wunderlich, 1928.
Czapski-Erdmann, V. *Die Auseinandersetzung des gotischen Weltgefühls mit dem antiken bei Rainer Maria Rilke.* Jena, Frommann, 1927.
Ermatinger, E. *Die deutsche Lyrik in ihrer geschichtlichen Entwicklung von Herder bis zur Gegenwart.* Leipzig (no publisher given), 1921.
Errante, V. *Rilke (studio critico)* [and translation into Italian of Rilke's works]. Milano, Edizioni Alpes, 1930.
Faesi, Robert. *Rainer Maria Rilke.* Zürich, Leipzig u. Wien, Amalthea-Verlag, 1920.
Faust, A. "Der dichterische Ausdruck mystischer Religiosität bei Rainer Maria Rilke," *Logos,* Band XI, Heft 2, 1922.
Gansberg, X. *Religionsunterricht?* Leipzig (no publisher given), 1906.
Gasser, Emil. *Grundzüge der Lebensanschauung Rainer Maria Rilkes.* Bern, Haupt, 1925.
Hett, Hans. *Das Stundenbuch Rainer Maria Rilkes als Ausdruck des Willens zum Leben.* Leipzig, Alexander Edelmann, 1935.

HEYGRODT, ROBERT HEINZ. *Die Lyrik Rainer Maria Rilkes.* Freiburg i. B., Bielefeld, 1921.

Inselschiff, Das: Eine Zeitschrift für die Freunde des Insel-Verlages. Leipzig, Insel-Verlag, 1927.

JALOUX, EDMOND. *Rainer Maria Rilke.* Paris, Emile-Paul, 1927.

KASACK, H. "Rainer Maria Rilke," *Die neue Rundschau,* February, 1927.

KAWERAU, SIEGFRIED. *Rainer Maria Rilke und Stefan George.* Berlin, Curtius, 1913.

KEY, ELLEN. *Seelen und Werke.* Berlin, S. Fischer, 1911.

LEPPIN, P. "Der neunzehnjährige Rilke," *Die Literatur,* August, 1927.

MacINTYRE, C. F. "Der Gebrauch der Farbe in Rossettis Dichtung," *Jahrbuch der philosophischen Fakultät in Marburg,* Marburg, 1923.

MADERNO, A. *Die deutschösterreichische Dichtung der Gegenwart.* Leipzig, Gerstenberg, 1920.

MAHRHOLZ, W. *Deutsche Dichtung der Gegenwart.* Berlin, Wegweiser-Verlag, 1927.

MARTIN DU GARD, MAURICE. "Rainer Maria Rilke," *Les Nouvelles Littéraires,* 1927.

MEYER, R. M. *Die deutsche Literatur des XIX. Jahrhunderts.* Berlin (no publisher given), 1906.

MICHEL, WILHELM. *Rainer Maria Rilke: "Apollo und Dionysos."* Stuttgart, Junker, 1904.

MICHEL, WILHELM. *Rainer Maria Rilke.* Berlin, Junker, 1909.

MONDT, E., UND HECHT, G. *Rainer Maria Rilke.* Leipzig, Engle, 1912.

MUSIL, R. *Rede zur Rilke-Feier in Berlin am 16. Januar, 1927.* Berlin, Rowohlt, 1927.

NAUMANN, H. *Die deutsche Dichtung der Gegenwart (1885–1923).* Stuttgart, Metzler, 1923.

NORTON, M. D. HERTER. *Letters to a Young Poet.* New York, W. W. Norton & Co., 1936.

OLIVERO, FEDERICO. *Rainer Maria Rilke.* Cambridge, W. Heffer & Sons, Ltd., 1931.

OPPELN-BRONIKOWSKI, FRIEDRICH VON. "Von Rilkes Art u. Kunstübung," *Mitteilungen der Literarhistorischen Gesellschaft Bonn,* Band II, Dortmund (no date).

PONGS, HERMANN. *Das Bild in der Dichtung.* Marburg, Elwert, 1927.

ROCKENBACH, MARTIN. *Rilke.* M.-Gladbach. Orplid-Verlag, 1927.

ROPS, DANIEL. *Carte de l'Europe.* Paris, 1927.

SCHAEFFER, ALBRECHT. *Rainer Maria Rilke.* Leipzig, Insel-Verlag, 1921.

SCHAEFFER, ALBRECHT. *Dichter und Dichtung.* Leipzig (no publisher given), 1923.

SCHELLENBERG, E. L. *Rainer Maria Rilke.* Leipzig, Verlag für Literatur, Kunst und Musik, 1907.

SCHNEIDER, F. J. *Der expressive Mensch und die deutsche Lyrik der Gegenwart.* Stuttgart, Metzler, 1927.

Scholz, Heinrich. *Rainer Maria Rilke: Ein Beitrag zur Erkenntnis und Würdigung des dichterischen Pantheismus der Gegenwart.* Halle, 1914.

Schwiefert, Fritz. *Rainer Maria Rilke.* Strassburg, Heitz, 1913.

Strich, Fritz. *Dichtung und Zivilisation.* München, Meyer & Jensen, 1928.

Susmann, Margarete. *Das Wesen der modernen deutschen Lyrik.* Stuttgart, Strecker & Schröder, 1910.

Thummerer, H. *Rainer Maria Rilke.* Prag (publisher not given), 1912.

Ullmann, Regina. *Von der Erde des Lebens.* München, Frauenverlag, 1910.

von der Leyen, F. *Deutsche Dichtung in neuer Zeit.* Jena, Diedrichs, 1922.

von Schlöser, L. "Rainer Maria Rilke," *Die Literatur,* March, 1927.

Wagner, Fr. *Rainer Marie Rilke.* Berlin-Wilhelmersdorf, A. R. Meyers, 1910.

Walzel, O. *Die deutsche Dichtung seit Goethes Tod.* Berlin, Askanischer Verlag, 1920.

Wernick, Eva. *Die Religiosität des Stundenbuches von Rainer Maria Rilke.* Berlin und Leipzig, De Gruyter, 1926.

Zech, Paul. *Rainer Maria Rilke.* Berlin, Borngräber, 1913.

Zech, Paul. *Rainer Maria Rilke: Ein Requiem.* Berlin, Officina seprentis, 1927.

Zweig, Stefan. *Abschied von Rilke.* Tübingen, Wunderlich, 1928.